KU-083-171

THOMAS COOK
Travellers

NORMANDY

HALLE AUX VIANDES

1784

BY
KATHY ARNOLD & PAUL WADE

Produced by AA Publishing

Written by Kathy Arnold and Paul Wade
Original photography by Rob Moore

Edited, designed and produced by AA Publishing.
Maps © The Automobile Association 1995, 1999.

Distributed in the United Kingdom by AA Publishing, Norfolk House, Priestley Road, Basingstoke, Hampshire RG24 9NY.

The contents of this publication are believed correct at the time of printing. Nevertheless, the publishers cannot accept responsibility for any errors or omissions, or for changes in the details given in this guide or for the consequences of any reliance on the information provided by the same. Assessments of attractions, hotels, restaurants and so forth are based upon the author's own experience and therefore descriptions given in this guide necessarily contain an element of subjective opinion which may not reflect the publisher's opinion or dictate a reader's own experiences on another occasion.

We have tried to ensure accuracy in this guide, but things do change and we would be grateful if readers would advise us of any inaccuracies they may encounter.

First published 1995
Revised second edition 1999
Reprinted 2001

© The Automobile Association 1995, 1999.

All rights reserved. No part of this publication may be reproduced, stored in a retrieval system, or transmitted in any form or by any means – electronic, photocopying, recording or otherwise – unless the written permission of the publishers has been obtained beforehand. This book may not be lent, resold, hired out or otherwise disposed of by way of trade in any form of binding or cover other than that in which it is published, without the prior consent of the publisher.

ISBN 0 7495 1882 0

A CIP catalogue record for this book is available from the British Library.

Published by AA Publishing (a trading name of Automobile Association Developments Limited, whose registered office is Norfolk House, Priestley Road, Basingstoke, Hampshire RG24 9NY. Registered number 1878835) and the Thomas Cook Group Ltd.

Colour separation: BTB Colour Reproduction, Whitchurch, Hampshire.
Printed and bound in Grafiasa, Porto, Portugal

Front cover: *Honfleur harbour;* Back cover: *Beuvron-en-Auge; Mont-St-Michel;* Title page: *meat market, Bayeux;* Above: *shop front, Ste Suzanne*

AA World Travel Guides publish nearly 300 guidebooks to a full range of cities, countries and regions across the world. Find out more about AA Publishing and the wide range of services the AA provides by visiting our Web site at www.theaa.co.uk.

Contents

About this Book

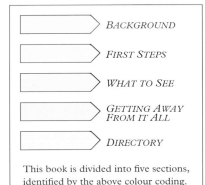

> BACKGROUND

> FIRST STEPS

> WHAT TO SEE

> GETTING AWAY FROM IT ALL

> DIRECTORY

This book is divided into five sections, identified by the above colour coding.

Background gives an introduction to the region – its history, geography, politics and culture.

First Steps offers practical advice on arriving and getting around.

What to See is an alphabetical listing of places to visit, interspersed with walks.

Getting Away From it All highlights places off the beaten track where it's possible to relax and enjoy peace and quiet.

Finally, the **Directory** provides practical information – from shopping and entertainment to children and sport, including a section on business matters. Special highly illustrated features on specific aspects of the region appear throughout the book.

Sunset on the chalk cliffs at Etretat, north of Le Havre

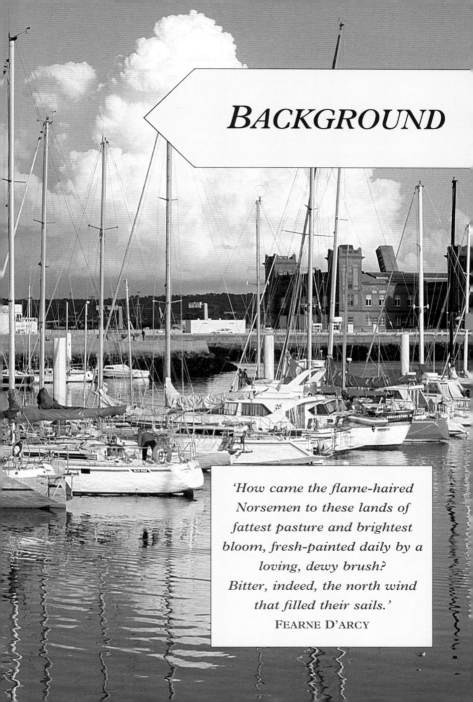

BACKGROUND

'How came the flame-haired
Norsemen to these lands of
fattest pasture and brightest
bloom, fresh-painted daily by a
loving, dewy brush?
Bitter, indeed, the north wind
that filled their sails.'
FEARNE D'ARCY

Introduction

From the 11th to the 13th centuries, Normandy, the coastal region lying to the northwest of Paris, was a powerful state in northern France. Peopled by hard-working, stubborn and conservative Scandinavians, it produced William, Duke of Normandy, and came to represent law and order, great castles and church builders. Despite being absorbed into France in 1449, then losing its status as a separate province after the French Revolution, Normandy is still recognised as a special area.

Normandy is now split into five *départe-ments*: Manche, Calvados, Orne, Eure and Seine-Maritime. After the ravages of World War II, nearly 600 towns had to be rebuilt; today, despite unemployment, there is still an overall look of affluence to the market towns and cities.

For some, the straight-from-the-sea fish and shellfish are good enough reason to visit; for others it's the pork and lamb, the rich cream sauces and renowned cheeses. Some come on pilgrimages: to Lisieux, and its basilica of the modern Saint Theresa; to Giverny, the home and gardens of the Impressionist painter Claude Monet; or to the D-Day beaches

NORMANDY LOCATOR

where family and friends fell in the Battle of Normandy in 1944.

French families come for their summer holidays as they have for nearly two centuries, ever since sea-bathing became fashionable. Thousands head inland, where small farms in peaceful, wooded valleys are a strong reminder of their roots. Then there are the cultural tourists, whisked by bus from the glory of Mont-St-Michel to the Bayeux Tapestry and on to Rouen's epic cathedral.

To savour the real Normandy you must drive the back roads, cycle on lanes through the *bocage* (hedged fields), shop in a market, stroll along cobbled streets and admire a small church. Then, you can discover the character and fascinating history of this distinctive part of France.

NORMANDY REGIONAL MAP

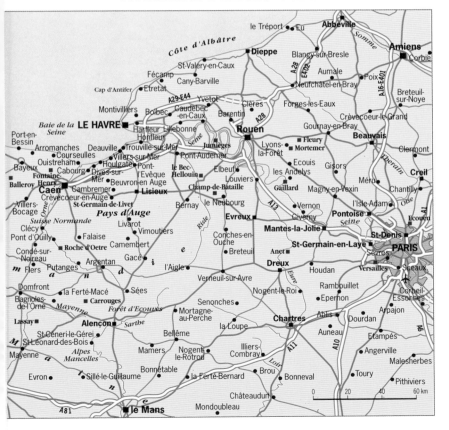

History

900 BC

The Celts move into what is now Normandy.

56 BC

Roman Conquest: Savinius defeats local chieftain Viridorix. As Roman rule strengthens, towns like *Mediolanum* (Évreux) and *Noviomagus* (Lisieux) develop, with *Rotomagus* (Rouen) as the capital of the region.

2nd to 3rd centuries

Christianity arrives, thanks to saints like Martin and Germanus among others. Many Norman villages still bear their names.

486

As the Roman Empire collapses, the Franks move in. King Clovis takes over Rouen and Évreux. Later his son Clothaire rules the Western Kingdom of Neustria.

6th to 8th centuries

Monasteries are built in the Seine valley; the network of monastic communities grows in size, influence and wealth. St-Wandrille Abbey is founded in 649, Mont-St-Michel in 708.

841

Rouen is burnt to the ground by the Vikings whose raids have become bolder, attacking first the coastal settlements, then sailing up the River Seine to Rouen and beyond.

911

Normandy, as we know it, is created by the Treaty (no more than a handshake) at St-Clair-sur-Epte. Rollo, Hrølf the Walker, becomes the first Duke of Normandy. Soon after, serfdom is abolished.

1027

The birth of an illegitimate son, William, to Robert the Magnificent, Duke of Normandy, also known as the Devil. Aged seven, the boy succeeds his father; William the Bastard becomes duke and, later, William the Conqueror.

1066

William invades England, defeats King Harold at the Battle of Hastings and is crowned King of England.

1087

William dies in Rouen and is buried in the Abbaye aux Hommes he founded in Caen.

12th to 15th centuries

The kings of France and England fight over Normandy. Since the Conquest, English monarchs own the Duchy of Normandy; their marriages bring them more French territory and even a claim to the French throne.

1152

After marrying Eleanor of Aquitaine, King Henry II of England rules one-third of France as well.

1259

In the Treaty of Paris, King Henry III renounces his claim to Normandy.

1337

Start of the Hundred Years' War with England.

1431

Joan of Arc is burned at the stake in Rouen.

1450

End of the Hundred Years' War. Thanks to King Charles VII's victory at Formigny on 15 April, Normandy is finally ceded to France.

1517

To strengthen France's international communications, King François I commissions the new port of Le Havre at the mouth of the River Seine.

1589
Protestant King Henry IV of France defeats the Catholics at Ivry-la-Bataille, near Évreux. The Wars of Religion are ended by the Edict of Nantes, 1598, which grants limited but significant rights to Huguenots (Protestants).

1608
Samuel de Champlain sails from Normandy to found Québec.

1682
Cavalier de la Salle of Rouen claims Louisiana for King Louis XIV of France, after sailing down the Mississippi River.

1685
The Edict of Nantes is revoked; thousands of Protestants involved in business and industry flee Normandy, leaving the area impoverished.

1789 to 1793
The French Revolution. Thereafter, the province of Normandy ceases to exist, replaced by five *départements*. Turbulent years follow: the Chouans (Royalist Normans) revolt but are crushed. The abbeys are closed, their stones quarried for use elsewhere.

1806
Sea-bathing becomes 'fashionable'; the coastal resorts begin to develop. Later, the railways accelerate the growth.

1825
The first regular cross-channel ferry between Normandy and England links Dieppe and Newhaven.

1870
Franco–Prussian War. Prussian soldiers occupy parts of Normandy and Le Mans.

1872
Monet paints *Impression: Soleil Levant* at Le Havre and exhibits it in Paris in 1874; the Impressionist movement is born.

1914–18
World War I.

1939–45
World War II. France is attacked for the third time in 70 years. The Germans occupy Normandy.

1944
6 June: the D-Day landings in Normandy begin the Liberation of Europe.

1994
The Pont de Normandie, a 2.1km bridge with a central span of 865m, links Le Havre with the Autoroute across the River Seine.

1997
The Tour de France starts in Rouen to commemorate local hero Jacques Anquetil, five-time winner of the race.

Normandy's hero: William the Conqueror on the attack in Falaise

THE NORMANS

SEAFARERS

A thousand years ago, the adventure-loving Vikings of Scandinavia sought new territory for their growing population. In their *drakkars* (longboats) they pillaged every estuary around the North Sea and beyond. After the death of Charlemagne, King of the Franks, Normandy presented a soft target and, in 841, these Norsemen, Northmen or Normans as they came to be called, sailed up the River Seine to pillage Rouen. By 911, their attacks were so frequent that King Charles the Simple of France gave in to Hrølf (Rollo). With the Treaty of St-Clair-sur-Epte, Normandy was exchanged for Viking allegiance, conversion to Christianity and a promise to halt further attacks. Some of these invaders stayed and names like Dieppe, Caudebec and Langrune (deep, cold-stream and

Above: fishermen at St-Vaast-la-Hougue
Left: doorway with faces, Brucheville

green-land) are a legacy. In later centuries, the Normans were to colonise parts of the Mediterranean, Africa and the New World.

MINORITY RULE

The swift transformation from colony to kingdom between 911 and 1066 is quite remarkable. In a mere 150 years, rampaging invaders turned into highly organised Frenchmen. Rollo and his companions were Norwegians who moved in as the ruling class. Soon Danes took advantage of their fellow Scandinavians' good fortune to move into the towns but the bulk of the population were still Franks. It was the invaders who gave up their pagan beliefs to embrace Frankish Christianity, the invaders who enforced local laws and the invaders who slowly abandoned their native tongue in favour of French. By the time that Duke William (himself a bastard) fought at the Battle of Hastings, his people were called the Franci or French as Panel 53 of the Bayeux Tapestry records.

Above: scene from the Bayeux Tapestry
Right: the Conqueror's tomb, St-Etienne

THE MOST FAMOUS NORMAN OF ALL

The Normans were a dynamic people, full of ideas and strong on organisation. Even today, they are regarded as the 'lawyers of France' for their love of rules and regulations. The high point of Norman civilisation came in the 11th century under William the Conqueror (see page 61), an excellent soldier, a clever legislator and a charismatic leader.

A LAND OF WAR

After William became King of England in 1066, Normandy was ruled by English kings off and on until the end of the Hundred Years' War in 1450. Then, there were religious struggles, since the Normans, like their Protestant fellow northern Europeans, were in conflict with the Roman Catholics. Many Normans supported the monarchy after the French Revolution of 1789, leading to yet more strife. Following the Revolution, the province of Normandy disappeared, to be replaced by five *départements*. Yet, 200 years later, the people of this area still think of and call themselves 'Norman'. Duke William would have been proud.

NORMANS TODAY

The outsider would find it impossible to distinguish 'Normans' from other French people: they dress, eat and drive much the same, even if they consume more cream and butter than the rest of the country. They tend to be a little reserved, but a smile and a handshake is usually enough to break the ice. 'In the south of France, they are more open, make lots of promises ... which they never keep,' as one Norman summed it up, 'whereas we take our time about whether we'll do something. But we'll never break a promise.'

Geography

*F*rom Mont-St-Michel on the Brittany border to Rouen is 245km; more specifically, some three million Normans live in an area about the same size as Belgium, whose population is three times larger. The Normans themselves talk about Haute (Upper) and Basse (Lower) Normandy. Roughly speaking, 'Haute' refers to the area bordering the River Seine, centred on Rouen; the rest is 'Basse'. Coastal Normandy contrasts with inland, while the whole is sliced by rivers ranging from the internationally known Seine to smaller waterways like the Eure and Orne, the Dives and Touques. In this book Normandy is divided into four areas.

Northeastern Normandy
This includes Le Havre and Rouen and is bordered by the River Seine. The Caux (chalk) region has expansive sugar-beet fields and white coastal cliffs. Inland are the vast beech forests of Eawy and

The Suisse Normande looks and feels a lot different to 'typical' Normandy

Lyons, as well as the fertile meadows of the Seine valley, which produce fruits and berries.

Central Normandy
Think of half-timbered cottages, cows and apple orchards; you will find them in the Pays d'Auge, where every bend in the road produces another idyllic-looking scene. Around Caen the land is open and flat. To the south, limestone is quarried, then the land drops away to the hills of the Suisse Normande, with its small, almost hidden, wooded river valleys.

Western Normandy
The Cotentin Peninsula is an out-thrust of the Armorican Massif that also characterises Brittany. Houses huddle together, sheltering from Atlantic gales, yet Granville and Carteret are popular summer resorts. In the northwest corner, coastal bluffs drop down to the sea, but inland and southwards the landscape softens into the *bocage*, a patchwork-quilt of small fields seamed by dense hedges. Mont-St-Michel is a familiar sight, a natural outcrop of granite, while the southeast corner around Carentan is marshland, criss-crossed with dikes.

Southern Normandy and Le Mans
This extends past the traditional boundary to include Le Mans and the Alpes Mancelles (the Le Mans Alps), not snow-capped peaks but a forested roller-coaster of hills and dales.

The coasts
Normandy boasts 600km of coastline, including some evocatively named

Normandy ingredients at Ouistreham: pasture, cattle and mellow buildings

stretches: the Côte d'Albâtre (Alabaster Coast) between Etretat and Dieppe; the Côte Fleurie (Flower Coast) from the River Seine to the Orne, with Trouville and Deauville; and the Côte de Nacre (Mother-of-Pearl Coast), where sand and sea shimmer in shades ranging from silver-blue to grey-green.

Vantage points

Two hills claim to be the highest point in western France, both near Alençon. To the west is the Mont des Avaloirs in Mayenne; northwest is the signal station in the Écouves Forest: both are 417m high. Tiny lanes criss-cross the countryside, often without signposts at intersections. Guess which turning to take and remember that getting lost is half the fun.

Climate

With the Atlantic Ocean to the west, the prevailing winds are the moist, mild southwesterlies. The intense green pastures result from cool, wet winters and mild summers with a regular sprinkling of rain.

Flora and fauna

There is more to Normandy than just cattle and horses. Some forests harbour roe and red deer; you will hear tits, thrushes and warblers, joined by nightingales and woodpeckers.

In spring, purple orchids and yellow primroses colour hedges, while the fields glint with cowslips. On the Cotentin Peninsula, sea thrift and spurge provide a pink and green patchwork, sea holly grows spiky and dusty purple, while marram holds the sand dunes together. In autumn, shearwaters, gulls and gannets soar overhead on their way south; in the marshes round Carentan, waders and wildfowl alight to shelter in the reeds.

Normans Today

A century ago, two out of three Normans worked in the fields and it is all too easy to regard the Normandy of today as one big, happy farmyard. Now, however, six out of 10 Normans live in a town. Not that there are many big towns: Caen and Le Havre have populations of about 200,000; Rouen, with 400,000, is the largest city.

Geraniums brighten the stonework on a house in Lassay-les-Châteaux

A rural tradition

France is one of the world's leading exporters of food and Normandy produces over 10 per cent of the nation's wheat and 10 per cent of its beef. To do this, hedges have been pulled up and fields enlarged to take tractors and harvesters. The European Union demands greater efficiency; the Common Agricultural Policy is not expected to protect the small farmer for much longer.

Food from land and sea

Luckily, Normandy's reputation for farm produce of high quality stands the region in good stead. Ducks and geese, usually associated with southwestern France, are now reared in Normandy too. The demand for *pré-salé* lamb from the salt marshes is being satisfied by ever bigger flocks of sheep along the coast.

The wealth brought to Fécamp and Dieppe by Newfoundland cod may be only a memory but shellfish production (oysters, mussels, scallops) thrives in several small seaside towns. There are still 1,000 fishing boats and 4,000 fishermen hauling in 70,000 tonnes of fish and shellfish every year, often for processing in efficient, modern factory ships. The port of Le Havre is one of Europe's largest, handling 10 per cent of the continent's imports.

Industry past, present and future

In the 1950s, Renault and Citroën, Moulinex and Philips built factories in this rural region, so close to Paris. The recessions of the '80s and '90s hit these, as well as steel and shipbuilding, traditional heavy industries which are no longer competitive and are closing down. Hopes for future prosperity look to hi-tech businesses such as pharmaceuticals, electronics and nuclear research, often working alongside the universities in Caen and Rouen. Power stations produce more electricity than the region needs; the nuclear reprocessing plant at Cap de la Hague is a major employer on the Cotentin Peninsula.

Communication links

Improved transportation ranges from the Autoroute de Normandie to railways hooking into the TGV (high-speed

but, unfortunately, the results look shabby now. Improvements are being made, with pedestrianised areas, renovation of old architecture and the embellishment of parks and squares. Although French city-dwellers still love the picture-book Normandy·countryside, many are discovering the delights of 'city culture'.

Mill (still working) and miller at Bois Landon, near Beaumont-sur-Sarthe

trains) network; even the charming *bacs* (ferries) are being superseded by bridges spanning the River Seine. First came the pont de Tancarville, next the pont de Brotonne, now the 2.1km-long pont de Normandie from Le Havre to Honfleur, opened in 1994.

The Channel Tunnel is only two hours north of Rouen.

Changing ...

Normandy faces big challenges and the revival of urban centres is a priority. After the massive destruction of World War II, speedy rebuilding was necessary

Away from the beaches, visitors are keen to watch clogs being made or linen being woven.

... but still Norman

The rest of France considers the Normans to be almost English in their habits: they take great pride in their homes, are famous for their love of gardens and gardening, while towns and villages seem neater and tidier than in the rest of France. As people, 'we may be a little cold at first, but we warm up quickly', says one hotelier, who sees tourism as a vital part of the new Normandy.

Politics

Administration

In the 1980s, the highly centralised government structure was reorganised. Power was devolved to the grassroots though justice, education and health remain national responsibilities. In the next layer down, Normandy is one of 22 regions, which in turn are subdivided into 96 *départements*. The lowest levels are *communes*, 36,500 districts, each with a mayor.

The regions administer tourism, cultural heritage, industrial development and adult education; *départements* oversee social services and welfare while the *communes* handle environmental matters, building and planning.

Départements have identifying numbers, shown on car licence plates (the last two digits) and used for postcodes: Calvados 14, Eure 27, Manche 50, Orne 61 and Seine-Maritime 76. The traditional regions of Upper and Lower Normandy encompass Eure and Seine-Maritime (Upper), Calvados, Manche and Orne (Lower Normandy).

Political parties

France has five recognisable political parties. The RPR (Rassemblement pour la République) sprang from the old Gaullist party of General de Gaulle. It encourages privatisation, low taxes and business. The UDF (Union pour la Démocratie Française), right-of-centre, tends to work in coalition with the RPR. The PS (Parti Socialiste) has moved towards the centre (pro-Europe and pro-NATO) while the PCF (Parti Communiste Français) has slumped in popularity since World War II. The party that has received most publicity in recent years is the FN (Front National), the ultra-right-wing racist party led by Jean-Marie le Pen.

The Normans

Overall, Normandy leans to the right when it comes to politics, as the rural vote dominates: the two Conseils Généraux are right wingers. Even Rouen and Caen have right-wing councils despite being industrialised. However, three other cities have been Communist for decades: Le Havre, Dieppe and Évreux. Traditions are being overturned, though, with Le Havre swinging to the right. In the 1998 elections, Lower Normandy stayed with the moderate right-wingers. By contrast, Le Pen's FN won so many votes in Upper Normandy that the complex rules of proportional representation have resulted in a political gridlock.

Politics is a serious and passionate business in Normandy and throughout France

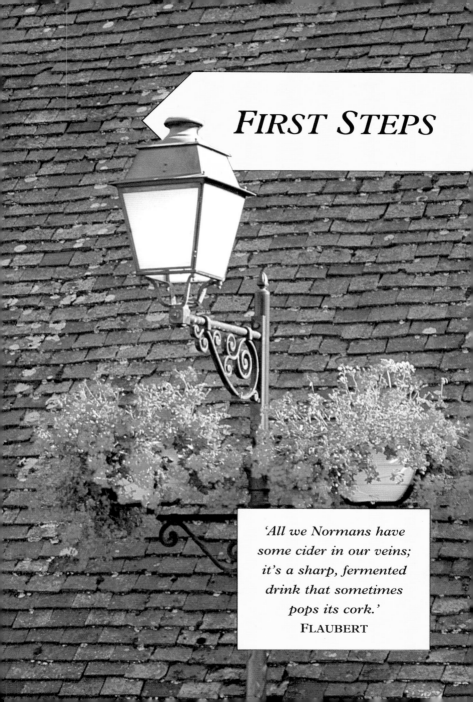

FIRST STEPS

'All we Normans have
some cider in our veins;
it's a sharp, fermented
drink that sometimes
pops its cork.'
FLAUBERT

Man-made Normandy

*A*lthough the inhabitants of the region are proud to trace their ancestry back to the Scandinavians, they are 100 per cent French. The shrug of the shoulders, the gesticulating hands, the familiar body-language are all on view. At the same time, there is often a feeling of old-time hospitality, where the foreign visitor is more of a guest than a tourist.

Arts décoratifs (decorative arts)

As well as the artists who drew inspiration from Normandy (see pages 50–1), craftsmen contributed to the cultural heritage of this region. In Dieppe and Fécamp the speciality skill was carving ivory; Alençon, Argentan and Bayeux were renowned throughout Europe for lace until the machines of Nottingham in England put paid to such labour-intensive hand-work. Rouen was a textile centre but it is faience that merits its own museum there. The tin-glaze on this earthenware provided a

Shingle towers of the church of St Catherine, Honfleur

sheen for floral patterns and, in the Revolutionary era, political sentiments. As for wood-carving, the *armoire de mariage* (wedding wardrobe) was more than just a cupboard for clothes: decorated with doves, fruit and flowers, this dowry gift was a work of art.

Castles

Fortifications abound in Normandy. Around every corner it seems there are souvenirs from the centuries of war: if the Normans were not battling against the English, then they were fighting their neighbours in Maine. These castles served as fortress, bank vault and home to the powerful administrators of the land.

Churches, cathedrals and abbeys

What astonishes the observant visitor is the individuality each master mason or architect managed to stamp on the standard cruciform design. Compare the bare simplicity of the church of St-Martin-de-Boscherville and the flamboyant swagger of St-Ouen in Rouen, less than an hour away. Or the elegant technology of the lantern tower on the nave of Coutances Cathedral (Gothic) and the neo-Gothic imitation surmounting the cathedral of Bayeux.

Some have stained-glass windows and tapestries, others delicate stonework and the gilded cups, boxes and regalia that were (and sometimes still are) used in religious ceremonies. Admire the

Founded in the 11th century, Arques-la-Bataille castle fell into ruined disuse 600 years later

grotesque carved faces hidden above pillars or among decorative leaves.

City sophistication

City-lovers enjoy the atmosphere of Rouen, where a modern public transport system sends suburban commuters into the cobblestoned heart of the largest city in Normandy. There are art galleries and concert halls, restaurants and antique shops and the glory of the great cathedral. Shopping is good, too, in Caen which has recently pedestrianised more of its old streets. Like Rouen and Caen, Le Mans has a university, which contributes to the artistic life and to the energy of the city.

Half-timbered houses

The half-timbering of Normandy comes in many colour combinations: brown against ochre, chocolate against pink, grey against white. Sometimes bricks add an extra dimension of pattern. While snug cottages with thatched roofs are classics of this style, surprisingly large houses were also built this way. Bayeux, the Auge region and even the old quarter of non-Norman Le Mans still have excellent examples of this type (see pages 66–7).

A variety of villages

From mere hamlets to bustling market centres, these communities are what visitors think of as typically Norman. Some are unattractive, straggling along main roads, so that the inhabitants have to wait for gaps in traffic to cross from the café to the *boulangerie* (bread shop). Others are almost hidden from view, tucked away in small valleys. The prettiest, such as St-Fraimbault in the Orne, are rated for their flowers, in gardens or window boxes. Many, like Bricquebec on the Cotentin Peninsula and Chambois near Argentan have huge impressive *donjons* (keeps).

WORLD WAR II

Much of Normandy was devastated by bombing, particularly before D-Day and then during the Battle of Normandy in the summer of 1944. The 50th anniversary of that invasion provided impetus for improving the displays and smartening up the image of many of the museums and monuments (see pages 86–9).

Natural Normandy

*P*ick up a large-scale map and lose yourself in the spider's web of tiny roads in the *bocage*, the tiny meadows with high hedges. Some have no signposts, and you could end up in a farmyard or back where you started. All are well paved even if narrow; single-track roads have passing places for cars and tractors. Travel by car and you travel too fast; travel by foot and you appreciate just how large Normandy is. Travel by bicycle, however, and you have the best of both worlds. On a *vélo* you can see over hedges, quickly find shelter in a sudden shower, and work up an appetite.

Beaches

Normandy does not have the blistering heat of the Mediterranean, but that can be an advantage for families with tiny

children. Certainly, there is plenty of sand for building castles, rock pools for discovering shrimp and seaweed to smell. Old blends with new: traditional beach huts still stand in a line while teenagers slice through the water on surfboards.

Cliffs

Not all of the Normandy coastline is flat sand. Chalk cliffs have been weathered into doorways at Etretat, but could have been sawn off by a giant near Dieppe. The Pointe du Hoc (see page 87) posed a stern challenge for the invasion forces on D-Day, while on the northwestern tip of the Cotentin Peninsula, drivers must take care not to be distracted by dramatic views as back roads suddenly twist or drop steeply downhill.

The seasons

In spring, Normandy's orchards explode into a snowstorm of apple blossom while hedges are spotted with wild flowers. In summer, caravan parks and camp sites fill with holidaymakers and the chic head for Deauville. Piles of yellowy-red apples fill orchards and the acid smell cuts through the autumn air as the fruit is crushed to make cider and calvados. As

Gentle greens and gentle slopes provide the themes for many Normandy landscapes

the leaves fall, country houses and mansions are no longer hidden from view. Dampness lends an extra chill to the air, and famous cathedrals and abbeys are as inviting as refrigerators, though at least the camera-toting hordes of summer have departed. Nowhere is worth a winter visit more than Mont-St-Michel. Photographers can sleep later and still snap the dawn light shining on the mount, while at night only a few people bother to walk the ramparts and explore the alleys which, without the crowds, are full of medieval atmosphere.

Huge, nearly empty, sandy beaches like this one north of Carteret are the best-kept secrets on the Cotentin Peninsula

THOMAS COOK'S NORMANDY

Cook started trips to the French coast in 1865, visiting Honfleur, Caen, Cherbourg, St Malo and other places 'of great historical interest to enlightened British travellers'. In 1882, John Mason Cook (Thomas's son) visited Normandy with a view to making arrangements for a new tour. In 1896, a personally conducted cycling tour of Normandy was advertised. This century, Normandy was a particularly popular seaside destination for British tourists in the 1930s, '40s and '50s.

Normans can seem taciturn, but most will treat visitors as welcome guests ...

THE PEOPLE

The best place to strike up a conversation – as long as there is no impatient queue behind you – is in a food shop. Ask about the breads and the flour-dusted baker himself may appear to point out his special six-grain bread or country loaf. Show interest in a *charcuterie* (delicatessen) and you may be given a taste of *pâté* and *rillette* or advice on what to buy for a picnic. Talk to a *fromager* and you could be discussing and comparing cheeses for hours. The Normans love their food, are proud of their food and talk a lot about it.

STANDARD OPENING HOURS

There is a bewildering variety of opening hours but in general everywhere is open daily during July and August. The problem is that some famous buildings are maintained by the state, others by the region, a few by the town and a handful privately. Each has different ideas about when to open. The major châteaux, churches and museums tend to open from 10am to 6pm, with two hours for lunch; most close for all or part of Monday or Tuesday. Ruined castles and abbeys are open during daylight hours, often until 7pm in summer but closing at 4pm in winter. Surprisingly, many are closed on national holidays. Basically, the more commercial the attraction, the more it is open. Do phone ahead when planning a specific outing, particularly if you want to join a guided tour. (See **Museums** on page 187.)

... and nearly all visitors will want to try Normandy seafood. This is an oyster bed

WHAT TO SEE

'This is paradise. There
can't be lusher meadows
or more beautiful trees.
The sea, or rather the
broad Seine, gives a
delightful horizon for these
grassy waves...'
BAZILLE
on the view from the Ferme St Siméon

Northeastern Normandy

*P*aris traditionally had two routes to the English Channel: overland to Dieppe, the nearest port, or via the River Seine. Between the two lies the flat Caux (chalk) plateau, broken by the wooded region of Bray and the beautiful beech forest of Lyons.

The importance of the River Seine was summed up by Napoleon: 'Le Havre, Rouen and Paris are but a single town of which the Seine is the main street.' Although this is a busy thoroughfare,

there are idyllic orchards, pretty villages and brooding castles on its banks. At the mouth of the river, *Le Havre* (the harbour) was built; Caudebec-en-Caux and Rouen were ports first developed for

NORTHEASTERN NORMANDY

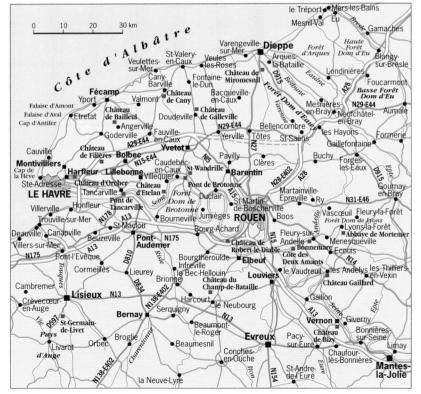

There are two natural arches on the cliffs at Etretat; this one is the Falaise d'Aval

sailing ships, then for steam-powered vessels.

This area of Normandy is full of history. Back in 1050, Duke William of Normandy persuaded Mathilda of Flanders to marry him at the border of their territories, the castle of Eu. This was replaced by a 16th-century château (now the Town Hall), lavishly redecorated by King Louis-Philippe 250 years later. On the coast, Fécamp and Dieppe were departure points for explorers claiming land and merchants buying goods for France.

Architectural heritage and the arts

Northeastern Normandy has plenty of variety and interest for the visitor beyond the spectacular coastal scenery of the towering chalk cliffs at Etretat, including museums, religious and military ruins, and the ancient city of Rouen with its magnificent cathedral, a monument to early engineers. Then there is Lyons-la-Forêt, a well-preserved village full of half-timbered houses, which is a touring centre for the surrounding woodlands. In medieval times, the lush water-meadows and mild climate of the Seine valley attracted monks who built some of the great abbeys of Europe: Jumièges, St-Wandrille and St-Martin-de-Boscherville.

The garden and ponds at Giverny modelled for some of Claude Monet's best-known paintings and further down the River Seine, at Villequier, a family tragedy inspired the heart-rending poetry of Victor Hugo whose house, like Monet's, is a shrine to enthusiasts. Flaubert based his notorious novel *Madame Bovary* on Ry, which is now the centre of a 'Madame Bovary' tourist industry. Another writer, Guy de Maupassant, spent his formative years in the Château de Miromesnil, near Dieppe, which perhaps triggered his jaundiced view of bourgeois society. Contemporary art is not forgotten: the 16th-century Château de Vascoeuil holds bold displays of modern sculpture, paintings and crafts.

Rouen

*J*oan of Arc burnt at the stake; the cathedral, painted by Impressionist Claude Monet; the Gros Horloge, the 16th-century clock in the old quarter: Rouen is different things to different people. The modern city sprawls along the banks of the River Seine, an unattractive muddle of docks and warehouses halfway between Paris and the sea. Its suburbs spread south to fill a huge bend in the river while the bright new university campus covers a hilltop to the north.

The lantern tower of St-Ouen's church soars over the rue de Miette

In Roman times, *Rotomagus* was a major administrative centre in Gaul. Later, Rollo the Viking, the first Duke of Normandy, dredged the river, built embankments and established a city that became the capital of Haute Normandie (Upper Normandy) and now the capital of the *département* of Seine-Maritime. Once the English were finally expelled in the 15th century, Rouen enjoyed a golden age, fired by the enthusiasm of

Cardinal Georges of Amboise who introduced Italian-influenced architecture. The extravagant Palais de Justice (law courts) is one legacy of the 16th century, when explorers and merchants sailed up the River Seine from Dieppe, Honfleur and Le Havre. The prosperity of the 17th century is exemplified by mansions such as the Hôtel d'Hocqueville, now the ceramics museum dedicated to faience, the French version of majolica, a tin-glazed earthenware.

Weaving was an important industry, though this suffered from the revoking of the Edict of Nantes (1685) which prompted the Huguenot (Protestant) traders and businessmen to flee, taking their technical know-how abroad. As ever, Rouen recovered and in the 18th century its textile industry added *rouennerie*, a coarse blue printed cotton fabric to its repertoire; then came twill and velveteen. The city's docks thrived, virtually a warehouse for Paris, and ranked among France's five largest ports, as they still do today.

In World War II, the Allies bombed the port and bridges, unfortunately badly damaging the strip between the river and the cathedral. The most important buildings were reconstructed and today Rouen looks lively with its high-quality shops. Wander from '*clocher en clocher*' (spire to spire) through the 6km of pedestrianised streets in the old town (see pages 48–9); discover the bust of Impressionist Claude Monet in the place St-Amand; and explore the Quartier St-Maclou, with its antique shops and the delightful rue de Robec, where half-timbered houses have tiny bridges across the small stream. To celebrate the year 2000, a new rapid transit system is being built and riverside areas are being cleaned up and redeveloped for housing.

Beautifully maintained houses help to make Rouen one of France's most attractive cities

ROUEN

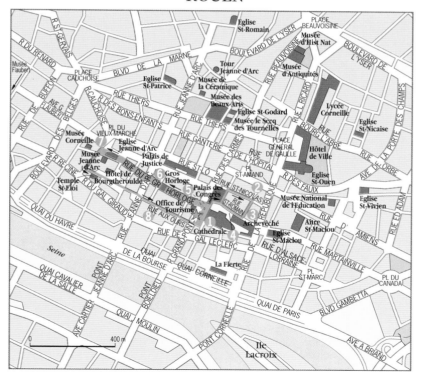

Intimations of mortality on Aître St-Maclou, a former charnel house

Aître St-Maclou

Look closely at the timber beams in this peaceful quadrangle: carved skulls, bones and shovels show that this was a warehouse for the bones of plague victims four centuries ago. Now it is the École des Beaux-Arts, the art college.
186 rue Martainville. Open: daily (see opening hours, page 22). Free.

Beffroi du Gros-Horloge

Six centuries old, the Great Clock still tells the time with a single hand, the day of the week indicated by the planets and phases of the moon (see page 49). The medieval mechanism is in the belfry where the Cache-Ribaud bell still rings the curfew at 9pm, as it has since 1260. You can climb the stairs

Rouen has many fascinating old buildings; the group called Gros-Horloge is particularly fine

for an unusual view of the old city.
Rue du Gros Horloge. Tel: 02 35 71 28 40. Open: Palm Sunday to September, Wednesday to Monday (closed: Tuesday, Wednesday morning). Admission charge.

JEANNE D'ARC (JOAN OF ARC)

When *La Pucelle d'Orléans*, the Maid of Orleans, was born a simple peasant girl in Lorraine in 1412, France was in disarray. The English and the Dukes of Burgundy controlled more territory than the crown; then, in the Battle of Agincourt (1415), King Henry V of England routed the French and retook Normandy. Charles VII, who succeeded to the French throne in 1422, remained uncrowned seven years later.

When visions of saints told the teenage Joan to rescue her country, few believed her, but she did not give up and eventually gained an audience with the king. He disguised himself in an attempt to trick her, but Joan was not fooled and persuaded him to allow her to lead an attack on the English at Orléans. Dressed in armour, she rallied the demoralised French and led them to a shock victory. The coronation of King Charles VII followed. A year later she was captured by the Burgundians who sold her to the English.

Joan's trial of heresy and sorcery was held in Rouen, which was still controlled by the English. Threatened with torture and death, she recanted, denying her visions and was sentenced to life imprisonment. The story goes that Joan had to promise not to wear men's clothes, but when she had to leave her cell for 'bodily necessities' only men's clothes were

Joan of Arc's execution spot in Rouen's place du Vieux Marché

available. Caught 'breaking her oath', she was sentenced to death.

On 30 May 1431, just 19 years old, she was burnt at the stake in the old market place. An ecclesiastical tribunal declared the trial illegal in 1456; 464 years later, in 1920, Joan was canonised. In World War II, the cross of Lorraine from Joan's native province was the symbol of the Free French.

Joan preparing for death at the memorial site in Rouen

The breathtaking artistry and technical skill of medieval masons on display at St-Maclou

Cathédrale Notre-Dame

Current renovation work on the cathedral is exposing the creamy-white stone of the west front and highlighting the montage of Gothic styles. The St-Romain tower on the left rises from 12th-century simplicity to 15th-century complexity and houses a 9.5-tonne bell, the Jeanne d'Arc. On the right, the Tour de Beurre, six layers of flamboyant stonework capped by an octagonal crown, has a 56-bell carillon. Soaring 151m is l'Aigle, the highest spire in France, topped by a red copper cockerel weighing 17kg ('the size of a sheep'). The changing light on this front was captured by Claude Monet in his series of 30 paintings (1892–4).

In the south ambulatory lies the stone effigy of Rollo, first Duke of Normandy, his robe drawn up under his arm. Near by are his son, William Longsword, and King Richard I of England. Nothing,

however, matches the 16th-century tomb of the Cardinals of Amboise in the Lady Chapel. They kneel humbly but are dressed in rich robes and surrounded by splendid carving. Light pours in through the lantern tower above the altar and stained-glass windows. On the north side, the 13th-century legend of St Julian the Hospitaller reads like a strip cartoon, from bottom to top. Tradition says this inspired Flaubert to write his story about St Julian. Certainly, the cathedral provides a romantic setting for the lovers in his novel *Madame Bovary*.

Photographs on the south side show how bombs disembowelled the cathedral on 19 April, 1944. Luckily, two flying buttresses held, preventing the whole nave from collapsing.
Place de la Cathédrale. Open: daily (see opening hours, page 22).

Église St-Maclou

Photographs inside show how World War II bombs all but flattened this fine example of flamboyant Gothic archi-tecture. The west front is crowned with a lacy, stonework tiara, while below, five 15th-century portals – and modern pigeons – greet visitors. The three central doors portray a sobering vision of the *Last Judgement*, though much of the carving needs renovation, as does the rest of the church, which only re-opened in 1980.
Place Barthélémy. Open: daily (except Sunday morning). Closed: January to April.

Église St-Ouen

This former Benedictine abbey church is badly in need of cleaning. Begun in 1318, it owes the continuity of Gothic style to Alexandre and Colin de Berneval, father

and son, who strictly followed the plans of the abbot, Jean Roussel. Music lovers can enjoy the acoustics and the 19th-century Cavaillé-Coll organ.
Place Général de Gaulle. Open: daily (Wednesday, Saturday and Sunday only in winter). Closed: Tuesday and mid-December to mid-January. Free.

Musée des Beaux-Arts (Museum of Fine Arts)

This museum is worth a visit just to see one of Monet's famous studies of Rouen Cathedral among the Impressionist works and Old Master paintings. One of 15 national museums set up in 1801, this old building was recently beautifully restored.
Place Verdrel. Tel: 02 35 52 00 62. Open: Wednesday afternoon to Monday (see opening hours, page 22). Closed: Tuesday, Wednesday mornings. Admission charge.

Musée de la Céramique (Ceramics Museum)

Strictly for fans of porcelain, this collection of Rouen faience is housed in the 17th-century Hôtel d'Hocqueville. In Room 15, *'Vivre libre ou mourir'* ('Live free or die') is just one of the uplifting messages on plates, bowls and jugs from the Revolutionary period.
1 rue Faucon. Tel: 02 35 52 00 62. Open: see Musée des Beaux-Arts. Admission charge.

Musée Flaubert et Musée d'Histoire de la Medécine (Flaubert Birthplace and Museum of the History of Medicine)

In 1821, author Gustave Flaubert was

> **GUSTAVE FLAUBERT (novelist) 1821–80**
>
> Flaubert would sometimes spend days writing just one page; no wonder it took him five years to write *Madame Bovary* (1857), his tale of a bored country wife in search of excitement. Charles and Emma Bovary were based on real people: Eugène Delamare, a Rouen surgeon who studied under Flaubert's father, and his second wife, Delphine Couturier, who had several affairs then committed suicide. Some of Emma's character is also attributed to the poet Louise Colet, Flaubert's mistress. He lived most of his life at Croisset, near Rouen, and enjoyed popping the *bourgeois* bubbles of self-satisfaction and respectability.

born in this 18th-century mansion, next to the Hôtel-Dieu (hospital). His father was a surgeon, so alongside medical implements are Flaubert memorabilia including his famous (stuffed) parrot.
51 rue de Lecat. Tel: 02 35 15 59 95. Open: Tuesday to Saturday (see opening hours, page 22). Admission charge.

Rouen faience – fine examples from the Musée de la Céramique

Musée le Secq des Tournelles (Wrought-iron Museum)

Some intriguing locks on coffers, a complete banister and hundreds of keys are among 12,000 items installed in an old church.
Rue Jacques-Villon. Tel: 02 32 52 00 62. Open: Wednesday to Monday (see opening hours, page 22). Admission charge.

Palais de Justice (Law Courts)

Seat of the Normandy Parliament from 1514, this sports fancy Gothic stonework that looks like the inspiration for London's Houses of Parliament. Make for the left wing where Pierre Corneille, the dramatist-lawyer, would have climbed the vast staircase to the *Salle des Procureurs* or *des Pas Perdus*, an ancient courtroom. An 850-year-old Jewish synagogue was excavated under the cobblestones of the main courtyard in 1976.
Place Foch. Tel: 02 35 52 87 52. Open: Wednesday afternoon to Monday (see opening hours, page 22). Free.

Place du Vieux-Marché

Dominating the old market square is the swooping modern church dedicated to Joan of Arc, who was burnt at the stake here in 1431. A 20m-high cross marks the spot. Many original half-timbered buildings survive: some are restaurants, like La Couronne, claiming to be the oldest *auberge* (inn) in France. Next door, the Musée Jeanne d'Arc is a depressingly touristy waxwork summary of the saint's life and times.
Tel: 02 35 88 02 70. Open: daily. Closed: Monday in winter. Admission charge.

Tour Jeanne d'Arc

This tower with 4m-thick walls is all that remains of the fortress where Joan of Arc was held captive and threatened with torture. Climb 50 steps for the history of the castle, 37 more for a history of the area and a further 35 to the very top, then look down through the opening between the supporting corbels.
Rue du Donjon. Tel: 02 35 98 16 21. Open: Wednesday to Monday. Admission charge.

Place du Vieux-Marché: traditional market and bold new church dedicated to St Joan

South of Rouen is Maison des Champs de Pierre Corneille, country home of the dramatist

Nearby:
Château de Martainville

As well as housing a comprehensive review of Norman furniture and architecture, this 15th-century mansion has fine examples of jewellery and pottery, costumes and glass, with a typical farmhouse interior.
16km east of Rouen. Tel: 02 35 23 44 70. Château open: daily except Tuesday. Admission charge.

Maison des Champs de Pierre Corneille

Although the dramatist would feel at home with the furniture and books inside his country retreat, he would be horrified by the factories and suburbs that close in on this 17th-century, half-timbered house.
8km south of Rouen. Rue Pierre Corneille, Petit-Couronne. Tel: 02 35 71 63 92. Open: Wednesday to Monday (see opening hours, page 22). Closed: November. Admission charge.

Pavillon et Musée Flaubert

Flaubert was a perfectionist. He would walk under the lime trees repeating sentences from *Madame Bovary*, which he wrote in this riverside house. Only one wing remains, filled with mementoes.
Croisset, 5km west of Rouen. Tel: 02 35 36 43 91. Open: Wednesday afternoon to Monday (see opening hours, page 22). Admission charge.

PIERRE CORNEILLE (dramatist) 1606–84

Rouen-born Corneille's early works were tales of love and comedy, but, summoned to Paris by Cardinal Richelieu, he suddenly changed direction. With *Le Cid* in 1636, he began creating larger-than-life heroes and heroines forced to choose between honour and passion. Where Greek tragedians bemoaned man's inability to alter fate, Corneille argued that man could make his own destiny. Parisian theatre-goers loved his work, but Richelieu was alarmed and discouraged the playwright. Corneille, however, continued to write, breaking new ground for playwrights like Racine who followed, and earning the title 'founder of French classical drama'.

Petit Andely and the River Seine as seen from Château Gaillard

LES ANDELYS

The villages of Grand and Petit Andely boast royal and artistic connections. In peaceful Petit Andely, half-timbered houses face the church of St-Sauveur, constructed by King Richard I of England at the end of the 12th century. It survived the Revolution (as a store-house for iron and lead) and now draws music lovers because of its 17th-century organ.

Further up the Gambon River is much busier Grand Andely, with its banks, shops and market. Here, according to legend, Queen Clothilde turned water into wine for labourers building a monastery. That was in the 6th century; unfortunately, the memorial fountain desperately needs a face-lift now. By contrast, the elegant Notre-Dame church can be compared to Rouen Cathedral, albeit in miniature. Note the scenes of rural life sculpted round the stained-glass windows (1540 and 1560) on the north side of the nave and the three paintings by the unknown Quentin Varin, whose pupil was the famous 17th-century artist Nicolas Poussin. Poussin's painting *Coriolanus* hangs in a small museum near by.

38km southeast of Rouen, on the north bank of the Seine, on the D313. Musée N Poussin, rue Ste-Clotilde. Tel: 02 32 54 31 78. Open: afternoons, Wednesday to Monday. Admission charge.

Just above Petit Andely and dominating this curve of the River Seine is **Château Gaillard**. Built in one year (1196) at the command of King Richard the Lionheart of England, the combination of fort and moated redoubt set upon a cliff seemed impenetrable. However, in 1204, King Phillipe-Auguste's men filled the outer moat, blew up a tower and then scrambled into the inner courtyard through the lavatory outlets.

Tel: 02 32 54 04 16. Open: Wednesday

Even in ruins Château Gaillard dominates its surroundings

afternoon to Monday (see opening hours, page 22). Closed: mid-November to mid-March. Admission charge.

ARQUES-LA-BATAILLE

The battle of this name took place here in 1589 during the Religious Wars: Henri IV overcame the greater forces of the Catholic Duke of Mayenne when fog delayed action, allowing the king's superior cannons to gain victory. The hilltop castle's inner gate bears a carved record of the success. The fortifications date back to 1038.

8km southeast of Dieppe.

CAUDEBEC-EN-CAUX

For four centuries Caudebec was the capital of the Caux (Chalk) Region that fans out from Rouen to the coast (see page 53). A popular stop-over for pilots navigating boats up the River Seine, the town was regularly flooded by the *mascaret* (tidal bore) until this was tamed in 1965. All this is explained in the Musée de la Marine de Seine, where an old notice board outside still records the day's traffic on the river. A fire in 1940 left little of the old town except for some of the 14th-century fortifications, the Maison des Templiers, a rare example of a 13th-century private house, and the Church of Notre-Dame. Stained-glass windows depicting St George and the coat of arms of one Fulke Eyton are a reminder of the English occupation for 30 of the church's 100 years of construction. There is a lively Saturday market and, on Sunday afternoons, free organ recitals in the church.

35km northwest of Rouen, on the north bank of the Seine, on the D982. Musée de la Marine de Seine. Tel. 02 35 95 90 13. Open: afternoons daily (see opening hours, page 22). Closed: Tuesday, September to June. Admission charge.

CLÈRES, CHÂTEAU DE

Clères means just one thing to French families – the zoo. Set in the pretty Clèrette Valley, the 16th-century château on the edge of the village has provided a spectacular setting for wildlife since 1920. Birds and mammals roam free in the gardens and parkland: kangaroos and peacocks, antelopes and monkeys, cranes and flamingos.

16km north of Rouen, off the N27. Parc Zoologique. Tel: 02 35 33 23 08. Open: daily (see opening times, page 22). Closed: December to mid-March. Admission charge.

In the village, opposite the slate-covered market hall, is the **Musée d'Automobiles**, dedicated mainly to military vehicles from World War II. As well as armoured cars and tank engines, there are vintage cars; the oldest is an 1894 Panhard-Levassor. The museum is closed at present.

Tel: 02 35 33 23 02. Open: daily 9am–7pm. Admission charge.

Cranes are among the creatures that roam free at the Château de Clères

NORMAN MONASTERIES

Signs for *l'abbaye de* .... appear in towns, villages and on lonely country roads throughout Normandy. Most of these monasteries are in ruins, yet literally and figuratively, they were the foundation stones of Norman culture and power. The Benedictine monks who set up these communities over 1,000 years ago followed a disciplined creed: *Laborare est orare*, 'to work is to pray'.

Over the years, they developed medicine and mathematics, music and animal husbandry; they drained marshes and tamed forests. Where we have schools and hospitals, libraries and pioneers of industry, Normandy had monasteries and monks.

These establishments were at the heart of cultural life. Thanks to murals and carvings, we can see how the people dressed. With their ability to write, the monks were an invaluable component of the communication network, often carrying messages from one lord to another. In an unstable world they provided organisation, but

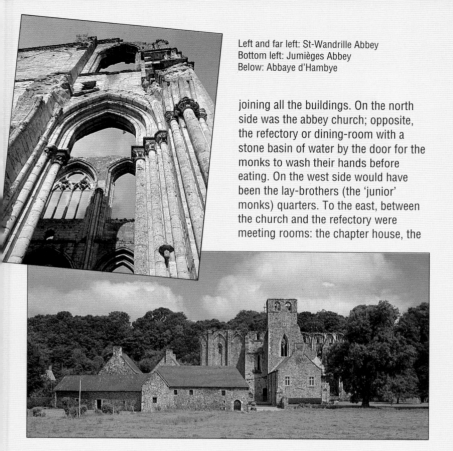

Left and far left: St-Wandrille Abbey
Bottom left: Jumièges Abbey
Below: Abbaye d'Hambye

joining all the buildings. On the north side was the abbey church; opposite, the refectory or dining-room with a stone basin of water by the door for the monks to wash their hands before eating. On the west side would have been the lay-brothers (the 'junior' monks) quarters. To the east, between the church and the refectory were meeting rooms: the chapter house, the

the wealth of the early settlements led to greed and many were plundered by the Vikings. William the Conqueror revived the power of the Church, using it as an arm of the government; his closest adviser was Lanfranc, a former prior of le Bec-Hellouin. The monasteries, with a new spirit of discipline, grew in power and influence.

The heart of monastic building was the garth or quadrangle, with a herb garden, important both for cooking and for making medicines. Surrounding this were the cloisters, a covered walkway

warming room and the day room. Above was the open dormitory shared by the monks. Outside, gardens and orchards were surrounded by a high wall for privacy and peace.

The outlines of many of these can be seen clearly today: at Jumièges and Hambye, St-Wandrille and le Bec-Hellouin. Sadly, after the monks were evicted during the French Revolution, many buildings were sold off as ready-made stone quarries. But their magnificence and their contribution to Western culture cannot be dismantled.

Dieppe

A dramatic facelift is improving this port, once badly run-down but now aiming to be a 'little Honfleur'. In 1994, a new terminal diverted ferry-bound cars and lorries from the *Avant-port*, now converted into a yacht marina. Having renovated the old Quartier St Jacques, the programme now includes the Bout du Quai (end of the quay), another warren of tiny lanes. Traffic-free streets like the Grande Rue bustle with shoppers, while cafés are extending on to the quayside. Behind the 2km of beach are tennis courts, a thalassotherapy centre and lawns where an international kite-flying competition is held biennially in September (even-numbered years).

Dieppe derives from the Viking word for 'deep' and for centuries this harbour was fought over by the French and English; the latter built the 12th-century castle but were finally ejected three centuries later. The 16th century saw Dieppe become a major port, whose 60,000 population was nearly twice that of today. Relays of horses rushed fish to Paris every night. Privateers captured booty in the Channel and eastern

> **THE BLOODY REHEARSAL**
> On 19 August, 1942, some 7,000 troops, mostly Canadian, raided Dieppe. 'Operation Jubilee' was a disaster, with over 1,000 Canadians and 113 RAF pilots killed and 4,000 troops taken prisoner. Because of this 'reconnaissance in depth', however, the Germans continued to believe that the inevitable invasion would be north of Dieppe, nearer Calais – an error which helped make D-Day a success.

Atlantic; their captain, Jehan, or Jean-Ango, is commemorated all over town. His fleet broke Portugal's control of routes round West Africa, allowing Dieppe traders to bring back spices, and ivory carved by local craftsmen.

In 1694, the Anglo-Dutch fleet razed the town, ironically, the home of Abraham Duquesne, chief of the French navy. As a Protestant, he could not be given the title of 'Admiral' but he does have a statue in the place Nationale. During the French Revolution, English

Altered and restored several times, the church of St-Jacques still retains brilliant Gothic detail

St Jacques, on the façade of the church in Dieppe dedicated to him

LITERARY LINKS

Oscar Wilde supposedly wrote *The Ballad of Reading Gaol* in the Café Suisse in the Arcades de la Bourse. Certainly, Georges Simenon of Inspector Maigret fame mentions it in *L'Homme de Londres*, set in Dieppe. The oldest pub is the 18th-century Café des Tribunaux (place Puits Salé), where the illustrator Aubrey Beardsley drank, as did painter Walter Sickert, who is said to have met Paul Gauguin there and advised him to give up art and stick to being a bank clerk.

skippers ferried aristocrats and clerics to safety; then, in the 19th century, Dieppe flourished as a holiday resort. French and British holidaymakers arrived by train and the regular ferry service was established in 1825. Lord Salisbury, the Foreign Secretary and later Prime Minister of Britain, even had a cross-Channel cable laid to maintain contact with London while on holiday.

Cité de la Mer

Opened in 1992, this hi-tech attraction teaches landlubbers about the sea, from steering by stars and satellite navigation to the formation of cliffs and model boats. Follow the career of a fish, from sea to dinner plate.
37 rue de l'Asile Thomas. Tel: 02 35 06 93 20. Open: daily. Admission charge.

Église de St-Jacques

There are cobwebs in the Jehan Ango oratory but this medieval church is being slowly restored. A memorial to the Canadians who died in the 1942 Dieppe raid is in a side chapel.
Rue St Jacques. Open: daily. Free.

Musée du Château

This well-preserved castle has local views by Impressionists Walter Sickert and Camille Pissarro, plus lithographs by Cubist Georges Braque who retired to nearby Varengeville. Take a look at the hand-carved ivory, especially the exquisite 18th-century figures, the *Four Seasons*.
Rue Chastes. Tel: 02 35 84 19 76. Open: daily (see opening times, page 22). Closed: Tuesday from September to May. Admission charge.

Ivory transformed by craftsmanship at the Musée du Château

BÉNÉDICTINE

While visiting the Benedictine monastery in Fécamp, a Venetian monk named Don Bernardo Vincelli wrote down his recipe for an elixir to cure the sick; that was in 1510. In 1863, Alexandre le Grand, a local wine-merchant, found the instructions in an ancient tome and reinvented the liqueur. Lemon peel, juniper oil, myrrh and saffron are among the 27 ingredients that, after a lengthy two-year process, result in Bénédictine. Now what was a cold cure is a world-famous *digestif* (after-dinner drink).

ETRETAT

The 19th-century author Alphonse Karr wrote: 'If I had to show a friend the sea for the first time, I would do so at Etretat.' Guy de Maupassant compared the Falaise d'Aval to 'a carved elephant dipping its trunk into the sea' while Maurice Leblanc used the 70m-high chalk needle as a hiding place for the stolen Mona Lisa in one of his *Arsène Lupin* books.

The towering cliffs, pierced by wind and waves to create *portes* (doorways), have fascinated man for thousands of years. The Romans built a road here from Lillebonne; Marie-Antoinette insisted on eating oysters specially raised here; and in the 19th century, the world and his wife came here by train for the casino and the theatre. The brave even went sea-bathing. Today, Etretat is no longer exotic. Camera tripods have replaced the easels of 19th-century artists Boudin, Corot and Manet, while the fishing community they painted is all but extinct. A few *caloges* (thatched cottages) rebuilt on the front are a reminder of yesteryear but even the handsome, beamed covered market dates only from 1926, having been moved here from Lower Normandy. Nevertheless, the cliffs remain truly awesome: the Falaise d'Amont (upstream) to the north, the Falaise d'Aval (downstream) to the south (see pages 54–5).
28km north of Le Havre, via the D940.

On the edge of town is the Château des Aigues, a 19th-century seaside palace for European aristocracy who came to spend 'the season' at Etretat. It houses a fine collection of Chinese porcelain.
Rue Offenbach. Tel: 02 35 28 92 77. Open: daily. Closed: Tuesday, except July to September. Admission charge.

FÉCAMP

Does the town's name derive from the Old German word *fisk* (fish), referring to the successful fishermen who dared even to cross the Atlantic for their catches? Or from *Ficicampum*, the place of the fig-tree? Supposedly, in the 1st century a hollowed-out fig tree was washed ashore, carrying drops of *Précieux Sang*, the Holy Blood of Christ, in a lead casket.

Certainly, Fécamp was a greater medieval pilgrimage site than even Mont-St-Michel. (A ticket for any of the three museums below gives a discount for the other two.)

A 15th-century ivory statuette of the Virgin in Fécamp's Bénédictine museum

General view of the museum in the Palais Bénédictine, Fécamp

Abbatiale de la Trinité

Behind the altar in this lovely abbey church a white marble tabernacle holds the *Précieux Sang*; to the right is a footprint marking the appearance of an angel to bishops in 943.

Rue des Forts. Tel: 02 35 28 84 39. Open: daily. Admission charge.

Musée Centre des Arts

This interesting, eclectic collection includes an assortment of baby's feeding bottles amassed by one Docteur Dufour, a crusader against infant mortality.

21 rue Alexandre-Legros. Tel: 02 35 28 31 99. Open: daily (see opening hours, page 22). Closed: Tuesday, September to June. Admission charge.

Musée des Terres-Neuvas et de la Pêche

Opened in 1988 to honour the *morutiers* (cod fishermen), this museum has displays about fishing and boat-building, nets and rescue services.

27 boulevard Albert 1er. Tel: 02 35 28 84 39. Open: daily (see opening hours, page 22). Closed: Tuesday, September to June. Admission charge.

Palais Bénédictine

From the outside, the Palais Bénédictine looks like a red-brick Disney fairy castle, with soaring spires. Inside, the serious business of making the world-famous liqueur continues in the huge copper stills. At the end of the tour there is a free tasting. There is also an art gallery and a museum here.

110 rue Alexandre-le-Grand. Tel: 02 35 10 26 10. Open: daily, mid-March to mid-November; mid-November to mid-March 10.30 only, afternoons. Admission charge.

Fécamp is 40km north of Le Havre, via the D925.

Nasturtiums below the pergola in Monet's gardens at Giverny

GIVERNY

This quiet riverside village has become a shrine to Claude Monet, who lived here from 1883 until 1926. The two-storey pink house retains his personal furniture, mementoes and fine collection of Japanese prints, but is spoiled by reproductions of his own works crammed on to some walls. Outside, the garden is still planted to the painter's design, while an underpass leads to the Oriental water-garden with its bamboo, weeping willows and water-lily ponds, which he also planned. Trying to savour the scene of the *Nymphéas* (water-lily) series can be disappointing when reality is a group of camera-toting tourists standing on the curved Japanese bridge. Arrive out of season, however, and the magic can still work.

Maison et Jardins de Claude Monet. Tel: 02 32 51 28 21. Open: daily, April to October. Closed: Monday. Admission charge.

Museé Américain

Opened in 1992, this low-profile museum examines the transatlantic connection inspired by Monet. He is shown in *The Wedding March*, painted by Theodore Robinson in 1892, following his stepdaughter and new American son-in-law, the painter Theodore Butler, down the (still recognisable) village street. There are several fine Impressionist-style works.

Rue Claude Monet. Tel: 02 32 51 94 65. Open: April to October. Closed: Monday. Admission charge.

Giverny is 76km west of Paris, in the Seine valley, off the D5.

LE HAVRE

Le Havre (meaning 'harbour') was built in 1517 to replace neighbouring Harfleur which had silted up. In 1944, eight days of intensive bombing flattened the city; clearing the rubble took two years. The Herculean task of post-war reconstruction was relished by Auguste Perret.

Now, however, Perret's love affair with concrete looks rather harsh: on the place de l'Hôtel de Ville, the town hall and its 72m-tall tower are dwarfed only by the 109m of the St Joseph Church bell-tower. Le Havre is one of Europe's largest ports; however, the attractive Ste-Adresse district to the west is the posh part of town where Monet grew up.

CLAUDE MONET 1840–1926
Born in Paris, Monet grew up in Le Havre where he met Eugène Boudin and was inspired to capture the atmosphere of the seaside. In the 1860s, Normandy was the cradle of Impressionism with Monet and friends meeting at the Ferme St Siméon in Honfleur, in Trouville and along the River Seine. They all were impressed by the shimmering, ever-changing light but it was Monet's *Impression, Sunrise* that gave the movement a name in 1874. Recurring themes are his gardens at Giverny and the west front of Rouen Cathedral. In his later years, when suffering from cataracts, his failing eyesight led to bigger and even bolder canvases such as the *Nymphéas* (waterlilies) series. However, his 'impressionistic' style was developed decades before.

Cathédrale Notre-Dame
Somehow this building managed to survive the bombing. Its eccentric mix of architectural styles puts Gothic and Renaissance cheek-to-cheek: a square, grey 16th-century bell-tower next to the warm, pink 17th-century portal.
Rue Ed Lang. Open: daily. Free.

Église St-Joseph
Minimalist on the outside, this Perret-designed concrete church comes to life inside, thanks to the brilliance of the stained-glass windows.
Boulevard François 1er. Open: daily. Free.

Musée de l'Ancien Havre
In a splendid 17th-century house in the oldest part of Le Havre, the history of the city is told. Apart from the architectural theme, one room is devoted to local folk music.
1 rue Jérôme Bellarmato. Tel: 02 35 42 27 90. Open: Wednesday to Sunday (see opening hours, page 22). Admission charge.

Musée des Beaux-Arts André Malraux
This is another striking building, offering a view of the sea through a concrete sculpture nicknamed the 'eye'. Inside are 200 paintings by the '*Roi des ciels*' (King of the Skies) Eugène Boudin, who encouraged the early Impressionists. Raoul Dufy, a Le Havre native, is also well represented.
Boulevard J F Kennedy. Tel: 02 35 42 33 97. Open: Wednesday to Monday (see opening hours, page 22). Admission charge.

Monet's studio at Giverny, with photographs of the artist

JUMIÈGES, ABBAYE DE

Tucked among fields on a bend of the
River Seine, this Benedictine abbey was a
centre of wealth and learning for 700
years (see page 53) until, after the
Revolution of 1789, it was blown up and
treated as a ready-made quarry. Now the
ruins, with the 27m-high nave open to
the sky, are hauntingly beautiful. The
west front, with its massive twin towers,
is a classic example of Norman building.
*27km west of Rouen, on the north bank of
the Seine, on the D143. Tel: 02 35 37 24
02. Open: daily. Admission charge.*

LYONS-LA-FORÊT

In the heart of the vast beech forest, this
photogenic cluster of brick, flint and
half-timbered houses centres on the
place Benserade (named for the 17th-
century poet born in Paris). Antiques
shops and *bistrots* look on to the medieval
covered market, supported by 27
wooden pillars. At the bottom of the rue
de la République on the right, a plaque
states that Maurice Ravel composed *Le
Tombeau de Couperin* (1917) and
orchestrated Mussorgsky's *Pictures at an
Exhibition* (1922) while living at Le
Fresne, a mock Norman house.

Château de Fleury

At the end of a parade of lime trees, this
17th-century pink-brick château has a
good collection of dolls.
*7km northeast of Lyons-la-Forêt. Tel: 02 32
49 54 37. Open: April to October, weekends; July and August, daily. Admission
charge.*

Château de Vascoeuil

More an arts centre than a château, this
fortified house exhibits contemporary
sculpture in the gardens and art in the
beautifully-restored *colombier* (dovecot).
A small cottage contains memorabilia of
the 19th-century historian Jules Michelet
who lived here.
*11km northwest of Lyons-la-Forêt. Tel:
02 35 23 62 35. Open: daily, afternoons.
All day June to August. Closed: weekdays
mid-November to mid-February. Admission
charge.*

*Lyons-la-Forêt is 35km east of Rouen, in
the heart of the forest, off the N31.*

MIROMESNIL, CHÂTEAU DE

Save this for a fine day, to enjoy the park,
formal gardens and restored kitchen
garden. The plain-looking chapel among

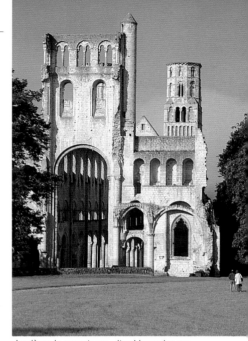

Jumièges is a must-see – its abbey ruins are beautiful and the setting is lovely

GUY DE MAUPASSANT (1850–93)
This great writer was born in Fécamp but spent his early years in the Château de Miromesnil, near Dieppe. He studied in Rouen and Yvetot, where he rejected religion. His relationships with women were unsuccessful and he became a pessimist. Maupassant's writing was nurtured by Gustave Flaubert and Émile Zola and his short story *Boule de Suif* was an overnight success in 1880. In all, he produced 300 short stories and six novels, most set in or about Normandy where he spent much of his time at Etretat. He died, aged 43, of syphilis.

beech trees reveals an ornate interior with painted statues and carved wood. Inside the 16th-century château are mementoes of Guy de Maupassant (see box) and statesmen such as Hue de Miromesnil, an 18th-century Chancellor of France.

Tourville-sur-Arques, 6km south of Dieppe, off the N27. Tel: 02 35 85 02 80. Gardens open: afternoons, May to mid-October. House open: daily, Easter to November. Closed: Tuesday. Admission charge.

PONT-AUDEMER

The River Risle divides to surround the old part of this thriving town, long famous for leather. Its nickname 'Normandy's Little Venice' may be an exaggeration but the fine 17th-century, half-timbered houses along canals crossed by wooden footbridges are distinctly romantic. Modern stained-

Half-timbered houses tumbling down the hill at Lyons-la-Forêt

glass windows complement 16th-century glass in the 11th-century Church of St-Ouen which remains unfinished after 500 years.

Just off the A13 motorway, 50km west of Rouen.

ROBERT-LE-DIABLE, CHÂTEAU DE

Somewhat touristy but amusing for children, the château exhibits a 20m *drakkar* (long ship), along with wax models telling the Viking story and the life of William the Conqueror. His father would hardly recognise the fortress he built, with the motorway above and the industrial port of Rouen below.

Near Moulineaux, just off the A13 motorway, 15km southwest of Rouen. Tel: 02 35 18 02 36. Open: daily, March to November. Admission charge.

RY

Called Yonville l'Abbaye in Gustave
Flaubert's novel *Madame Bovary*, this
undistinguished village has cashed in on
its literary connection. Emma Bovary
was based on Delphine Couturier, the
doctor's wife, who died in what is now
the chemist's shop. The pharmacy in the
novel is now the dry cleaners ... and Ry's
old chemist's is now in the Musée
d'Automates, many of whose 500
moving mechanical figures re-create
scenes from the book.
*20km northeast of Rouen, on the D13.
Galerie Bovary. Musée d'Automates, place
Flaubert. Tel: 02 35 23 61 44. Open:
Easter to October, Saturday to Monday,
also afternoons Tuesday to Friday in July
and August. Admission charge.*

Flower shop in Ry, a village made famous by its
connections with Flaubert's *Madame Bovary*

ST-MARTIN-DE-BOSCHERVILLE

Unlike the nearby ruined abbeys of St-
Wandrille and Jumièges, the Caumont
stone of St-Martin-de-Boscherville
shines brilliant-white, thanks to recent
renovation. Built originally for the
Augustinians, the abbey was taken over
by the Benedictines in 1114. They were
ejected during the French Revolution
and this impressive building is now the
parish church. The monastery garden is
being restored, while archaeologists have
found traces of a pagan temple dating
from 100 BC under the 12th-century
chapter house (see page 52).
*10km west of Rouen, off the D982. Tel:
02 35 32 10 82. Open: daily. Admission
charge.*

ST-WANDRILLE

To get the best out of a visit to this
abbey, take a tour with a Benedictine
monk (see page 53). Since St Wandrille
settled here around 650, communities
have come and gone. After the
Revolution, 100 years passed before the
monks returned; the present community
has lasted since 1931. At first glance this
looks like a château, but inside are the
skeletal ruins of the 13th-century abbey
church and the early 16th-century
flamboyant Gothic cloisters. The monks
worship in their 'new' church, a 13th-
century Norman tithe barn they took
down and reassembled in 1967. Even
non-believers are moved, listening to
Gregorian chants ringing out.
*30km west of Rouen, off the D982. Tel: 02
35 96 23 11. Open: daily. Guided tours
available. Telephone for times. Admission
charge.*

VALMONT

Only the Lady Chapel stands intact
among the ruins, but the delicate arches
and altarpiece of the Renaissance interior
retain their elegance. This Benedictine
abbey was founded by the Estouteville
family, made famous by Victor Hugo in
The Hunchback of Notre-Dame; their
ancestral home across the river features
a 900-year-old keep.

Filigree stonework and weathered statues on the façade of Rouen Cathedral

Just past rue St-Amand, turn right into an alleyway, the rue des Chanoines.

3 RUE DES CHANOINES

Barely two people wide, this passageway of dark corners and buckling walls evokes medieval Rouen. The backs of buildings reveal layers of architectural history in wood, stone, and slate shingles. High above soar the spires of the cathedral.
Turn right on to rue Saint-Romain, returning to place de la Cathédrale.

4 RUE SAINT-ROMAIN

On the Archevêché (Archbishop's Palace), one plaque recalls the trial of Joan of Arc in May 1431, another her rehabilitation by Cardinal d'Estouteville 25 years later. Admire No 74, a classic 15th-century house with a lion's head on the door, carved figures and leaded glass windows.
Cross the cathedral square and walk down the pedestrianised rue du Gros-Horloge.

5 RUE DU GROS-HORLOGE

Look above chain-store windows to appreciate the age of the houses. At the corner of rue du Bec, a plaque honours Cavalier de la Salle, who explored the Mississippi River and claimed Louisiana for France. Another plaque, on the old Town Hall (corner of rue Thouret), cites M Thouret, a *député* (represent-ative) of Rouen. The date is *14 brumaire an II*. In the Republican calendar introduced after the Revolution, *brumaire* was the second month of the year; the Year II was 1793.

The tomb of the two Cardinals Amboise in the Lady Chapel of Rouen Cathedral

6 GROS-HORLOGE

In 1527, locals had this highly-decorated clock lowered from the nextdoor belfry so they could see the single hour-hand and phases of the moon more clearly (see page 28).
Cross rue Jeanne d'Arc and continue towards the market square.

7 PLACE DU VIEUX-MARCHÉ

A tall cross, *la Croix de la Réhabilitation*, marks the spot where Jeanne d'Arc died (see pages 29 and 32). Today, small restaurants occupy the old buildings overlooking a stark, modern church whose design echoes a ship's hull.
Turn left on rue du Vieux-Palais, then left on rue Samuel Boshart. Cross the square to rue aux Ours.

8 RUE AUX OURS

This quiet street has a mixture of architectural styles. Note the medieval house by the ruined St Pierre du Chatel. Number 61 was the birthplace of François-Adrian Boïeldieu (1775–1834), composer of operas (*Le Calife de Bagdad, La Dame Blanche*). Number 46 was the birthplace (1785) of scientist Pierre Louis Dulong, whose research into heat resulted in Dulong and Petit's Law.
Return to the cathedral.

ARTISTS AND WRITERS

Over the centuries, Normandy has produced and attracted artists, writers and musicians. Many are national figures; others, such as Boudin (see page 73), Corneille (see page 33), Flaubert (see page 31), de Maupassant (see page 45) and Monet (see page 43) have international reputations.

WRITERS

Canon Wace of Bayeux (1120–83)
Canon Wace was the first writer to use everyday French. His *Roman de Brut* reinforced the legend of King Arthur, while the *Roman de Rou* described early Norman history.

Alexandre de Bernay (11th century)
This wandering troubadour, whose poem about Alexander the Great (1,952 lines long) followed a 12-syllable line metre, gave rise to the 'alexandrine' verse metre used centuries later by Corneille and Racine.

Victor Hugo (1802–85)
France's greatest 19th-century poet spent many years in Normandy and fought for the region when he was in parliament. The 1980s hit musical, *Les Misérables*, was adapted from his book; his moving poem, *A Villequier* was inspired by the death of his daughter (see page 47).

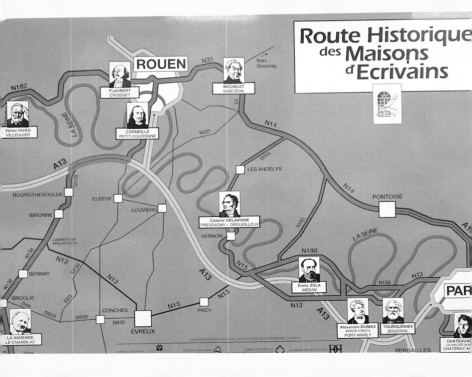

Route Historique des Maisons d'Ecrivains

Left: route map to writers' houses in the Seine valley
Right: painting by Monet

Alexis de Tocqueville (1805–59)

De Tocqueville, a brilliant politician from the Cotentin peninsula, is remembered for his incisive analysis of democracy in America and the French Revolution.

Marcel Proust (1871–1922)

Having spent childhood holidays in Cabourg, Proust wrote about Normandy in many of his award-winning novels. Cabourg, for example, is the Balbec of *À l'ombre des jeunes filles en fleurs*.

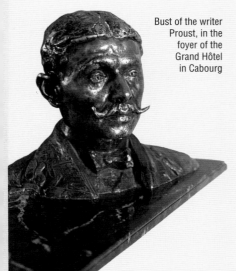

Bust of the writer Proust, in the foyer of the Grand Hôtel in Cabourg

ARTISTS

In addition to Monet and Boudin, Renoir, Seurat, Pissarro and Sisley also painted profusely in Normandy, known as the birthplace of Impressionism, at Honfleur and Le Havre.

Jean-François Millet (1814–75)

The Norman countryside often features in landscapes by this son of a peasant from the Cotentin peninsula. Sentimental scenes like *Les Glaneuses* (*The Gleaners*) make popular living-room prints today, but he was condemned as a 'socialist' in his later years.

Fernand Léger (1881–1955)

From the same peasant background as Millet, the innovative Cubist has a surprisingly low profile in his home town of Argentan. Near Lisores, his farmhouse sports a boldly-coloured mural of a milkmaid and cow.

The Banks of the Seine

The River Seine has long been a major transport route. This drive traces a quiet loop, where industry is absent but there is history behind every wall. *Allow half a day.*

Leave Rouen on the D982 following signs for Canteleu. The road affords spectacular views over the River Seine. At St-Martin-de-Boscherville, turn left to the Abbaye St-Georges.

1 ST-MARTIN-DE-BOSCHERVILLE

Such a massive abbey in so small a village is a surprise (see page 46). Careful restoration is returning the massive walls of the abbey to its 11th-century glory.
Return to the D982, following signs for Jumièges and Duclair.

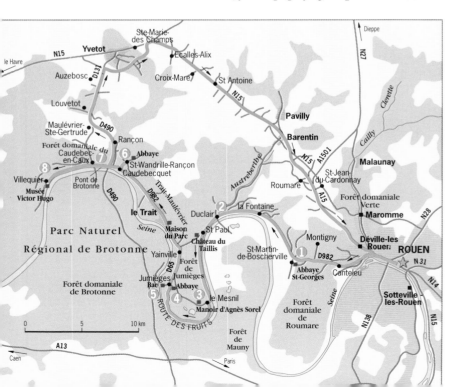

2 DUCLAIR

After driving through orchards and past ancient barns, the River Seine reappears on the left. Enter the Parc Naturel Régional de Brotonne and the straggling hamlet of Duclair, known for its ducks. Here the *bac* (ferry) takes cars and foot passengers 100m across the river.
Just beyond Duclair, turn left on to the D65 towards le Mesnil.

3 LE MESNIL

Spot the garages built into the cliff behind thatched cottages. Gnarled trees in orchards produce Melrose, Jonagold and Golden Delicious apples. La Maison de l'Abeille (The World of Bees) is a small apiculture farm outside Mesnil, known for its 700-year-old manor house where Agnès Sorel, the influential mistress of Charles VII, died in 1450, aged 28.
Continue towards Jumièges on the Route des Fruits.

4 JUMIÈGES

A high stone wall on the right announces Jumièges (see page 44). The twin towers of the 7th-century Benedictine abbey still dwarf the houses at its gate. Legend recalls the *énervés*, the princes whose hamstrings were cut in punishment for rebelling against Queen Bathilde in the 7th century and who sought asylum here.

5 BAC

If there is time, drive down to the *bac* landing station where a small *auberge* is a peaceful spot for refreshment while admiring the cliffs across the Seine.
Return to the main road, which rejoins the D982. Turn left towards le Trait but watch carefully, once the Pont de Brotonne (Brotonne Bridge) comes into view, for the sign to St-Wandrille on the right, the D22.

6 ST-WANDRILLE

The huge, ornate, wrought-iron gate could be a château's entrance but this is an abbey (see page 46). Outside the walls is the village church which dates from the 11th century.
Return to the D982 and turn right for Caudebec.

7 CAUDEBEC-EN-CAUX

On the right, almost in the shadow of the Pont de Brotonne, stands a monument to five brave, near-forgotten aviators – Guilbaud, de Cuverville, Dietrichson, Brazy and Valette. In 1928, they flew to the Arctic Circle to rescue Italian balloonists who had crashed near Spitzbergen. The Frenchmen, accompanied by the Norwegian explorer Amundsen, were lost without trace in their Latham 47, built at the aero factory near by which still functions. Away from the main road, the attractive heart of Caudebec centres on the medieval church of Notre-Dame and the Maison des Templiers (see page 35).
Continue on the D982; fork left to Villequier, beyond Caudebec.

8 VILLEQUIER

Houses crowd the bank in this attractive village which is synonymous with author Victor Hugo (see page 47). In a riverside park just before the hamlet, Hugo's statue stares sadly towards the spot where his daughter and son-in-law were drowned by the infamous *mascaret* (tidal bore) in 1843.
Turn round; return to Rouen via Caudebec, Yvetot and the N15.

La Maison de l'Abeille Tel: 02 35 91 36 76. Open: afternoons, April to November. Admission charge.

The Cliffs of Etretat

This is not recommended for those with a fear of heights or with small children. The paths have been etched into the chalk over centuries and have few or no safety railings, while at the top the cliff edge is crumbling away. That said, these are two invigorating walks: one south, the other north of the town. Sensible shoes are recommended. *Allow half an hour for each walk.*

Walk 1 – south to the Falaise d'Aval

1 PLACE VICTOR-HUGO
Start outside the Casino where the concrete promenade has been built to protect the town from the violent winter storms. *Turn left along the promenade.*

2 TERRASSE G COURBET

Glass windbreaks on all four sides protect the outdoor cafés from breezy weather. Even in winter, surfboarders cavort in the cold, grey waves. A Noah's Ark houses the local sailing club and every morning oilskinned fishermen sell *carrelet* (plaice), *cabillaud* (cod) and *barbue* (brill) caught only minutes before. Beware: some visitors head south along the beach towards the *porte* (gateway), heedless of large signs warning that tides can leave you stranded.
Continue along the promenade. Climb the steps up the cliff.

3 FALAISE D'AVAL
After 93 concrete steps, a flint-filled path, worn into the hillside, leads to the top (see page 40). Across the ravine to the left is a golf course. Bear right and, after 15 minutes, cross a narrow bridge to reach a small, rather grubby concrete

blockhouse. Paths, like white fingers, spray off to vantage points on the cliff edge. Now look back at the spectacular view across the bay that has attracted visitors for decades.
Return, but remember loose flints can make the downhill walk tricky under foot. Follow the promenade past the place Victor-Hugo.

Walk 2 – north to the Falaise d'Amont

_1_ TERRASSE E BOUDET
Pass the _boules_ court. Out to sea, stumps of collapsed cliffs protrude from the water. At the end of the promenade, climb 83 steps on the new concrete path, past a park.

_2_ CHAPELLE NOTRE-DAME DE LA GARDE
At the top is a little-used granite chapel, a 1950 replacement for the original, destroyed in World War II. The gargoyles are fun: each is a metre-long seal. Now look back to the south for another sweeping panorama across the bay, to the arch in the Falaise d'Aval, so often painted at sunset.
Follow signs to the Falaise d'Amont, a 10-minute walk.

_3_ FALAISE D'AMONT
If the Falaise d'Aval is terrifying, the Falaise d'Amont is humbling. A narrow cliff path cuts down to the sea, getting

> **Musée Nungesser et Coli**
> Tel: 02 35 27 07 47. Open: daily, Easter to end October. Admission charge.

ever narrower. Sadly, visitors cannot resist carving their names in the chalk, which is layered with flints. At least there is a wooden handrail here with a ladder for the final descent to the beach where the water churns remorselessly at the base of awesome cliffs.
Return to the clifftop and the chapel.

The heads of airmen Coli and Nungesser on their memorial at Etretat

_4_ MONUMENT NUNGESSER ET COLI
Inland from the sailors' chapel is a car park and a needle-like memorial that is part bird, part Concorde, marking the efforts in 1927 of Nungesser and Coli, two aviators lost trying to fly the Atlantic.

_5_ MUSÉE NUNGESSER ET COLI
This museum is a tribute to the two aviators.
Return to the promenade via the stairs.

Central Normandy

*C*entring on Calvados, the *département* that gave its name to a famous drink, this is the Normandy everyone recognises: dairy-rich meadows and renowned cheeses, the glamour of Deauville and the romance of Honfleur, cradle of Impressionist art. It is also William the Conqueror country: born in Falaise, buried in Caen.

This area is renowned for its famous cheeses, many named after the places they come from – Camembert, Livarot and Pont-l'Évêque. Camembert is less than a hamlet, while Livarot and Pont-l'Évêque are small towns, sweeter smelling than their eponymous products. Nowadays, most of these are factory-made but you can visit farms where *lait*

cru (unpasteurised milk) produces the full flavour that one French gourmet described as 'kissing the feet of God'.

Deauville is like a theatre without a play for much of the year, until the summer when the rich and famous, *paparazzi* and budding starlets turn the *planches* (promenade) into a cabaret – no wonder the down-to-earth prefer

CENTRAL NORMANDY

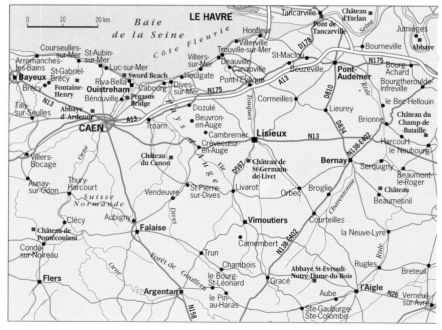

Trouville, next door. Cabourg is snooty and sophisticated, remembering its past as Marcel Proust did in his writing about his childhood holidays here. To the west, the resorts would be unremarkable were it not for *Jour J* (D-Day), a turning point in world history (see pages 86–9) recorded in a string of small museums.

If Honfleur wins the 'prettiest harbour' prize, then Beuvron-en-Auge merits 'prettiest village' over other rivals in the Pays d'Auge region. Expect crowds on weekends and in summer. The châteaux of Crèvecoeur-en-Auge and St-Germain-de-Livet are straight out of fairy tales.

Le Bec-Hellouin was once the intellectual and spiritual heart of

The Conqueror's castle at Caen

Normandy thanks to the clever monks at its abbey. Lisieux, a thriving town with two open-air markets is one of the world's great pilgrimage centres: Ste Thérèse, whose photograph appears all over Normandy, came to live here in 1877.

Brionne, with its ruined keep, and Flers in the Orne valley are just two places that produce a 'this is the real France' reaction from visitors. Don't expect to ski in the Suisse Normande, the rolling hills and valleys south of Caen; but have a go at canoeing and hanggliding, mountain biking and hiking.

With a castle, two abbeys and an exquisite church, Caen has one foot planted firmly in the past, but the lively university and the replacement of old industry with high technology ensures the other foot is in the future. Between the two is the Mémorial, museum for peace.

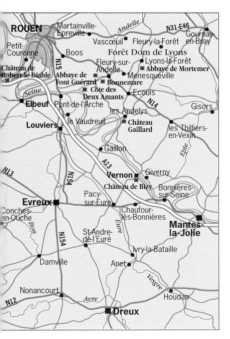

Caen

' ... the most prepossessing, ... and most happily situated of towns. Its streets are the handsomest, its churches, public buildings and walks the finest of their kind; and from this town have come the brightest wits and intelligences of their country.' So wrote diarist Madame de Sévigné in 1689 and though such praise may smack of public-relations hype, the capital of the Calvados *département* is today a balance of glorious monuments and post-World War II construction. But Caen is a city that prefers to look forward, investing heavily in the technology of tomorrow. Between Caen and Hérouville-St-Clair, north-west of the city, is Synergia, a hi-tech industrial park. GANIL, the Grand Accelerateur National d'Ions Lourds, is an international research project into how matter is made, using a heavy ion accelerator.

CAEN

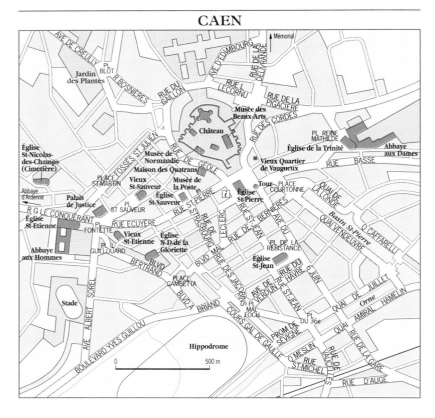

CAEN STONE

The creamy whiteness of Caen limestone gives it the appearance of being too soft for building material, yet it has created magnificent monuments not just in France but also in England. Caen stone was floated down the River Orne and across the English Channel for use in the cathedrals of Canterbury and Winchester as well as Westminster Abbey.

When King Henry V reoccupied Normandy in 1415, he commandeered the quarries solely for building his royal palaces. In World War II, caves dug into the sides of these limestone pits south of the city sheltered locals from bombing.

became King of England rebellion led to battles. The English were expelled in 1204, only to return in 1346 when King Edward III's troops filled a hundred boats with booty from the looted city. After the French defeat at Agincourt in 1415, it took 33 years to get rid of the English '*Goddons*', presumably named for the soldiers' expletives.

Caen's links to the sea are the River Orne and the 12km-long canal to Ouistreham, developed by Brittany Ferries as a ferry port. Join locals at the lively Friday farmers' market in the place St-Sauveur and the rue St-Pierre, walk in the old town (see pages 78–9) or visit le Mémorial, the hi-tech museum of peace with its park, created for the 50th anniversary of D-Day in 1994. This is located on the northwest side of the city.

Caen's population of 150,000 includes 22,000 students at the university which is best known for its faculties of science and French literature. The students add to the liveliness of the city, especially on a Thursday night in the pubs and cafés around the campus. Students come from all over Europe to attend the Centre Chorégraphique National, to train as dancers.

Long the chief city of Basse Normandie, the old Lower Normandy of pre-Revolutionary days, Caen was the favourite town of William the Conqueror, whose massive castle is the focal point, positioned halfway between the great abbeys built by him and his wife as penance for breaking the rule forbidding cousins to marry. After he

Nos 52 and 54 rue St-Pierre, superb early 16th-century timbering and detail

Abbaye aux Dames

The façade of the abbey church, l'Église de la Trinité, looks a little strange, thanks to some fanciful restoration in the mid-19th century. Its towers were reduced to their stunted state during the Hundred Years' War. Next door, the convent buildings are now council offices. Once inside, however, all is much as William and Mathilda would have seen it during its consecration, with the recently-cleaned Caen stone the colour of heavy cream. The arches look heavy and masculine, with only geometric carvings for decoration, but close examination of the capitals reveals grotesque faces as well as recognisable animals such as a heron and frog.

Glowing Caen stone on the convent buildings of the Abbaye aux Dames

Visit the church in the morning, if possible. On sunny days, a blood-red light streams through the stained glass, dramatically illuminating a simple black marble slab on the chancel floor, the tomb of Queen Mathilda.
Rue des Chanoines. Tel: 02 31 06 98 98. Guided tours: daily 2.30pm, 4pm. Free.

Abbaye aux Hommes

William was finally laid to rest in the Church of St-Etienne, twice as long and twice as wide as la Trinité. Today, houses crowd up against its walls and the stark west front is almost lost in the small square off rue Guillaume-le-Conquérant. The Hôtel de Ville (Town Hall), formerly the 18th-century monastery, abuts the south side and only from its gardens can the scale of this church be appreciated.

WILLIAM THE CONQUEROR (1027–87)

'Stark he was ... so harsh and cruel ... that none withstood his will; all men were obliged to be obedient, and to follow his will, if they would have lands or even life.' So the *Anglo-Saxon Chronicle* described William the Bastard, born of a romantic alliance that is legendary (see page 72). He became Duke of Normandy at the age of seven and by 20 was a battle-hardened leader. At Domfront, he challenged Geoffrey Martel, Count of Anjou, to personal combat; the Count backed down. When the citizens of Alençon mocked him, jeering 'Tanner' from the walls, he cut off the hands and feet of 32 offenders after capturing the city.

William invaded England after the death of King Edward the Confessor. As the king's cousin, his claim to the throne preceded that of Harold, who was only Edward's brother-in-law. Several years before, William had tricked Harold into swearing on holy relics to respect the Duke's right to the English throne. Short, muscular and with a vile temper, William was also far-sighted and just, a harsh but efficient administrator who gave his barons land in exchange for their loyalty, cleverly spreading these assets across the country to prevent any ideas of 'empire-building'.

William was happily married for 30 years to his cousin, Mathilda of Flanders, but grew ever more greedy, ruthless and fat. Injured in a 'skirmish' with the French king, the Conqueror died in Rouen in 1087, at the age of 60, the most famous Norman of all.

Now part of Caen town hall, the monastic buildings of the Abbaye aux Hommes

It was built in 11 years, with money appropriated from a conquered England; seven spires mark the spot where construction began in 1066. The high interior gives a tremendous feeling of space and repairs over the centuries have been in keeping with its austerity. When the wooden roof of the nave was rebuilt in stone in 1130, the Gothic vaulting was kept simple, and when the lantern tower collapsed in 1566, the prior, Dom Jean de Baillehache, copied the original. In World War II, the church suffered little in the long battle for Caen; thankfully, the Resistance had managed to alert the Allies that hundreds were sheltering inside.

Rue Guillaume-le-Conquérant. Tel: 02 31 30 42 81. Open: daily. Guided tours: 9.30am, 11am, 2.30pm, 4pm. Admission charge.

Le Château

The remains of William's 11th-century castle never fail to impress. Within the massive walls and towers are public gardens and museums: the 900-year-old Echiquier (Exchequer), now beautifully restored, holds temporary exhibitions, as does the tiny Chapelle St-Georges. Picture this back in 1418, crowded with a dozen knights ready to receive the Order of the Bath from King Henry V of England.

Musée des Beaux-Arts

Reopened after a major face-lift, the museum's highly-rated collection of 16th- and 17th-century art is now properly lit and chronologically arranged. Classic 19th-century seaside scenes such as Courbet's *La Mer à Langrune* and Boudin's *La Plage de Tourgéville* are found among works by Monet, Vuillard, Bonnard and Dufy.
Tel: 02 31 85 28 63. Open: daily (see opening hours, page 22). Admission charge.

Cider press and copper still (for calvados) in the Musée de Normandie

Musée de Normandie

This fascinating 'then' and 'now' explanation of Norman life is in the handsome Logis des Gouverneurs (Governors' Palace). Maps prove that Roman roads are still main routes; models contrast the 'open' farmyards of the Cotentin Peninsula with the 'closed' design around Argentan. Half-timbering with stone, brick and wood is demonstrated and there are cider presses and copper stills for making calvados. Admire the stunning wedding dress of '*blonde*' (ivory silk) lace, discover what a *tyrossemiophile* is, but don't miss the grave of a blacksmith surrounded by his tools.
Tel: 02 31 86 06 24. Open: Wednesday to Monday (see opening hours, page 22). Admission charge.

Église St-Pierre

Traffic rumbles round this church whose exterior desperately needs cleaning. Inside, the flamboyant Renaissance stone-carving is remarkable, particularly the capitals of the second and third pillars on the north side of the nave, where Sir Lancelot and Sir Gawain, knights of the round table, accompany munching rabbits in a field of cabbages.
Rue Montoir-Poissonerie.

Le Mémorial

A jagged split in the smooth white façade is just one symbol of the 20th century's *faillité de la paix*, the failure of peace. This ultra-modern memorial-cum-museum has aroused much controversy. Does it over-dramatise war? By selling models of warplanes and T-shirts with doves, does it become 'just another tourist attraction'? Decide for yourself.

Inside, a Hawker Typhoon aircraft hangs over a pile of rubble from Caen, 'the martyred city'. A spiralling ramp leads down into chaos: Fascism and Communism rise; Wall Street crashes; screens blaze with the torches of

Complex vaulting in one of the side chapels of Église St-Pierre

Nuremberg rallies. Next, darkened rooms emphasise the Depression and progression into war. The plight of the Jews is movingly portrayed with individual stories personalising the horrifying statistics. Most significant for the French, however, is the question: '40 million collaborators – 40 million resisters?' The self-examination accuses the French militia of being the 'zealous arm of the occupying power'.

Then, suddenly, you are in a conventional museum of World War II, with guns and uniforms, maps and models, plus relics and films of the Battle of Normandy. The research centre focuses on the war and there is a gallery dedicated to Nobel Peace Prize winners. *Avenue du Maréchal Montgomery. Tel: 02 31 06 06 44. Open: daily. Admission charge.*

Musée de la Poste et des Techniques de Communication

A long name for a small museum of postage stamps and communications, from the telegraph to the telephone. *54 rue St-Pierre. Tel:*

02 31 50 12 20. Open: mid-June to mid-September, Tuesday to Saturday; afternoons only rest of the year. Admission charge.

Vieux Quartier de Vaugueux

All of Caen once looked like this cluster of tiny, cobbled streets east of the castle. The ancient houses are now a United Nations of restaurants.

Exhibits in the Mémorial-Musée pour la Paix

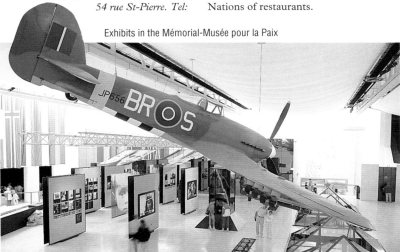

Lining up for paradise – the six noble lords of Aubigny

ANET

Never underestimate the charm of an older woman. Henry II was just a 12-year-old prince when he fell under the spell of Diane de Poitiers, the beautiful 32-year-old widow of the powerful Lord of Anet. Although Henry married Catherine de Medici, his mistress Diane effectively ran France for over a decade. The 'queen without a throne' lavished attention on Anet in the mid-1500s, transforming it into an Italianate palace with huge courtyards and formal gardens on the banks of the River Eure.

Architect Philibert Delorme, who designed the Tuileries, Fontainebleau and Chenonceau, rated Anet his finest work. The best tiles and tapestries along with sculpture by masters such as Benvenuto Cellini completed the magnificence. Unfortunately, much of the complex was pulled down in the early 19th century, but one wing and a chapel are open to the public. Note the gatehouse: above the clock stands a stag at bay, surrounded by four dogs which would have moved when the clock struck.

Tel: 02 37 41 90 07. Open: April to October, afternoons daily (except Tuesday); Saturday, Sunday afternoons in winter. Admission charge.

Ivry-la-Bataille

Just across the river, the name recalls the victory of Henri IV over the Duke of Mayenne and the Catholic League in 1590. The King supposedly stayed at 5 rue de Garennes. The church of St-Martin, with its splendid tower, is another Diane de Poitiers/Philibert Delorme venture.

Anet is on the River Eure, 16km north of Dreux on the D928.

AUBIGNY

Just north of Falaise on the N158 is this small village, known for the six Lords of Aubigny. These life-sized statues kneel facing the altar in the chancel of the church, their (sculpted) clothes reflecting their times – from 1625 to 1786. Note the expectant smile on number five, unlike the devout expressions of the others.

BEAUMESNIL, CHÂTEAU DE
This soft-pink brick and stone baroque extravagance is a 17th-century mini-palace, complete with formal gardens and moat. Owned by the Furstenberg Foundation, it is known for its library of 17th- and 18th-century tomes and a museum recording the history of book-binding.
13km southeast of Bernay. Tel: 02 32 44 40 09. Grounds open: Wednesday to Monday. Château open: Easter to September, Friday to Monday afternoons; July, August, all day, except Tuesday. Admission charge.

BEC-HELLOUIN, LE
The sleepy air of 'Le Bec' belies its role in history. In 1042, Lanfranc, an Italian intellectual, joined the monastic community, transformed it into a seat of learning and became Archbishop of Canterbury after the Conquest of England in 1066. Bec's importance also grew: the abbey church was one of the largest in Europe, but was pulled down after the Revolution, like so many others. The 15th-century Tour de St-Nicolas remains, however, and the view over the Risle Valley from the top is worth climbing the 201 steps. The 18th-century dormitories were used by the army until 1948 when the Benedictine monks revived the place's religious heritage.
23km northeast of Bernay, on the D130. Tel: 02 32 43 72 60. Open: Wednesday to Monday (see opening hours, page 22). Admission charge.

Beuvron-en-Auge is genuinely picturesque and correspondingly popular

BERNAY
A busy, small town that escaped war-time bombing and deserves the label 'typical', Bernay is worth a stop to admire the 11th-century abbey church and carved façades on medieval houses in streets such as rue Gaston Follope, with its antique shops.
57km southwest of Rouen, on the N138.

BEUVRON-EN-AUGE
This picture-postcard village in the Pays d'Auge, with half-timbered houses on the main square, a covered market and a chapel, is famous for its cheese, cider and horses. Parking is difficult since this is a favourite destination in summer and on fine weekends.
30km due east of Caen, on the D49, between the N13 and the N175.

THE NORMANS

Although Norman castles, cathedrals and abbeys set new standards for monumental structures, the region also developed distinctive domestic architecture.

FARMHOUSES

The sea-going ancestry of the Norsemen is reflected in their farmhouses. The shape resembles inverted *drakkars* (longships), oriented east-west to get the maximum sunshine. Long and narrow, these thatched houses always

had the outside staircase at the sheltered east end; the west end, facing the prevailing wind, was shaped like the ship's prow. The irises planted along the roof ridge are more than mere decoration: the strong roots bind together the thatch with the clay inserted along the ridge as a seal.

Above: granite farmhouse near Avranches
Right: *colombier* (dovecot) at the Château de Vascoeuil, near Rouen

DOVECOTS

Colombiers (dovecots) were often the first target for destruction by mobs during the French Revolution because the feudal system permitted local lords to keep pigeons which gobbled up grain from the peasants' fields. Yet, the handsome, brick-built cylinders or octagons still dot the landscape. Many have been restored. Some are thatched, others tiled or covered in slate, and all have conical roofs. Since they provided fresh meat year-round, these were valuable assets. Some have chequerboard patterns of flint or glazed bricks; others have elaborately carved stone doorways, complete with coats of arms. All have a *larmier*, or ledge round the middle to stop rats and mice from climbing up and in. Inside were dozens of *boulins* (niches) for the pigeons and a rotating ladder for the keepers to collect eggs and birds.

MANOR HOUSES

Normandy's manor houses are a delight but since most are privately owned, few visitors see more than the intriguing exteriors. The end of the Hundred Years' War with England

AT Home

(1450) sparked a boom in building. Though the advent of the cannon made castles redundant, protection was still needed, but from brigands not armies. So, these houses have turreted towers, streams diverted into moats, little look-out posts hanging from corners, and gatehouses guarding courtyards. As the

years went on, these details became decorative rather than functional.

Top: in Beuvron-en-Auge
Above: typical half-timbered manor house in the Pays d'Auge

HALF-TIMBERING

Though common all over Europe, the Normans were particularly adept at half-timbering. Using an early form of pre-fabrication, frames could be assembled on the ground and then hauled up into position. They were often dismantled and reassembled if and when the owner decided to build on or move. The timber beams of the framework (*pans de bois*)

were filled in with wattle and daub (*hourdis*). Clay was often mixed with chopped straw or even cow dung for extra strength. The wood itself has lasted for centuries because it was properly cut and aged. Felled in late autumn or winter, the day after a full moon so that sap levels were right, the timber was left to dry out slowly.

Sunshine on the attractive avenue de la Mer, Cabourg

CABOURG

Popular with families, this resort on the Côte Fleurie boasts a 3km promenade. Once a simple fishing village, in 1860 it was redeveloped with streets radiating out from the Grand Hôtel and casino. Many *belle époque* buildings survive but Cabourg is best known as Marcel Proust's childhood holiday destination, renamed 'Balbec' in his novel *À l'Ombre des Jeunes Filles en Fleurs* (Within a Budding Grove). The annual Romantic Film Festival in June is great fun.
On the coast, 22km northeast of Caen.

CAMEMBERT

The village is not much more than a church, a few houses and a famous name. The Beaumoncel farm where Marie Harel lived is privately owned; a memorial stele on the D16 stands below the village (see opposite). Since 1992, the Maison du Camembert (shaped like a cheese box) has demonstrated the production of the cheese and sold examples from local farms, plus calvados and even dandelion jam.
3km south of Vimoutiers, on the D246. Tel: 02 33 39 43 35. Open: Easter to November, daily (see opening hours, page 22). Admission charge.

CHAMP-DU-BATAILLE, CHÂTEAU DE

Parisian owner Jacques Garcia spent two years restoring the splendour of this late 17th-century mansion château, reopening it in 1994. Admire the marble, tapestries and paintings, then stroll through the woods and parkland.
37km southwest of Rouen, off the D840. Tel: 02 32 34 84 34. Open: weekends, March to May, mid-September to mid-November; daily, May to mid-September. Admission charge.

CLÉCY

If you want to take a break from history, abbeys and châteaux, Clécy, in the heart of the Suisse Normande by the River Orne, is a centre for walking, canoeing, rock-climbing and hang-gliding.

Musée du Chemin de Fer Miniature (Model Railway Museum)

Children and fans of model trains enjoy 'Europe's largest miniature railway layout' with an airport and coal mine. There are some 180 locomotives and 500 trucks plus a short model train ride in the grounds.
Les Fours à Chaux. Tel: 02 31 69 07 13. Open: April to October, daily; Sunday

> **MARIE HAREL**
>
> A priest fleeing the Revolutionary mob took refuge in Camembert. In gratitude, he gave 'his' recipe for a Brie-like cheese to his protector, farmer's wife Marie Harel. She and her daughter (also Marie) improved and refined it; a grandson gained recognition when Napoleon III approved of the flavour and ordered more in the 1850s. That is the legend; but Camembert only became famous after M Ridel invented the circular chipwood box in 1890, enabling the cheeses to be shipped in quantity. Marie gets all the credit, however ... and two statues in Vimoutiers.

afternoon only in winter (see opening hours, page 22). Admission charge.

Clécy is 38km southeast of Caen, on the D562.

CONCHES-EN-OUCHE

This is another 'ordinary' Norman town with one of everything. In the 16th-century Church of Ste-Foy, which occupies the site of a church founded by Roger de Tosny after the Crusades, look for the 'Mystic Wine Press' in the fifth window in the south aisle. For atmosphere, visit the crumbling, overgrown ruins of the castle keep, dramatically floodlit in summer, and the Maison des Seigneurs, with its 800-year-old cellars once used as prison cells.
18km southwest of Évreux, on the D830. Maison des Seigneurs, 12 rue Sainte-Foy. Tel: 02 32 30 20 50. Open: Wednesday to

Home of one of the world's great cheeses (only eat when ripe!)

Sunday (see opening hours, page 22). Admission charge.

CRÈVECOEUR-EN-AUGE, CHÂTEAU DE

A stream meanders through manicured lawns surrounding an ochre and half-timbered manor house; geese and ducks splash in the water, children fish in the moat. It is all idyllic, except for the traffic whizzing by on the N13. This cluster of ancient buildings includes a chapel, gatehouse and dovecot. The owners made a fortune from their technique of using seismology to search for oil back in 1927. A museum about oil prospecting and modern art exhibitions contrast with the story of medieval architecture.
34km east of Caen, on the N13. Museum – tel: 02 31 63 02 45. Open: April to October, daily (see opening hours, page 22). Admission charge.

DEAUVILLE

Bette Davis, Elizabeth Taylor, Lee Marvin, Roger Moore, John Travolta ... the roll call of names by the cabins on the *planches* (boardwalk) proves this is, and has been, one of the world's great resorts. Yet Deauville hits the headlines of the society pages for only 14 weeks each summer (see page 152).

History records that the half-brother of Napoleon III, the Duc de Morny, decided to develop the sand dunes to the west of Trouville, aiming to build a posher version of that holiday spot. That was in 1860. For making Deauville a magnet for society-types, however, credit goes to Eugène Cornuché. In 1910, he built a casino, a racecourse and the 700m-long boardwalk on the wide beach, so the rich and famous didn't have to get their shoes sandy.

In recent years, Deauville has worked hard to maintain its up-market image: a new marina at the mouth of the River Touques, more flowerbeds, repaved squares and an even longer boardwalk. Forget the semi-seediness of some seaside towns: here buildings are strictly

The new marina at Deauville

regulated to conform to the 'traditional' half-timbered Norman style. But the beams come in red, blue and ochre as well as traditional brown and black, while the 'cottages' facing the ocean are sized in medium, large and giant, like the sprawling Hôtel Normandy next to the casino. To experience the *joie-de-vivre* that makes Deauville legendary, visit during 'the season'. That's when the stars of the gossip columns are shopping in the jewellers' and designer boutiques. Out of season, the shutters of houses and apartments behind the seafront are firmly closed and the atmosphere is muted but there are bargains, even at the priciest hotels. Deauville attracts visitors all year long; even in winter, a fine weekend brings promenaders to the boardwalk and champagne-sippers to the Bar du Soleil.

DIVES-SUR-MER

From here William of Normandy set off to conquer England in 1066. The names of 475 of the warriors who assembled here are on the west wall of the church of Notre-Dame in what is now just an ordinary seaside village.

22km northeast of Caen, on the coast.

Colourful corner in Dives-sur-Mer

DREUX

Dreux is busy but rather soulless, except
for the pedestrianised streets in the old
centre with its 16th-century belfry. The
castle here was pulled down in 1593 for
choosing the 'wrong' side against Henri
IV. Dreux had already been given to the
royal Orléans family, which explains the
tombs of exiled King Louis-Philippe and
family in the early 19th-century Chapelle
Royale St Louis above the town.
80km west of Paris, on the N12.

ECOUIS

In the Church of Notre-Dame, classical
music echoes from speakers under the
brick-vaulted ceiling. Among the notable
carved and painted wood panelling and

statues is a 14th-century statue of St
Agnes wearing a pleated gown worthy
of the couturier Fortuny. Find it on the
northwest wall of the transept. Realistic
carvings on the choir stalls include an
old man's head on a rat's body. Well
worth a stop.
*Off the D321 west of Fleury. Tel: 02 32 69
43 08. Open: daily. Admission charge.*

Nearby:
The Abbaye de Fontaine-Guérard, a
tranquil 12th-century ruin on the River
Andelle, is quite haunting at dusk.

37km southeast of Rouen, on the N14.

ÉVREUX

The ancient capital of the Eure is mainly
modern, with factories on the outskirts
but river-side walks and flowerbeds in the
centre. Ransacked, besieged and
bombarded for over 1,000 years, the few
survivors of the past include the Tour de
l'Horloge, a medieval clock tower whose
two-tonne bell is known as Louise; the
Cathédrale de Notre-Dame topped by
the Clocher d'Argent (silver bell tower);
and the Ancien Évêché (Old Bishop's
Palace).
53km south of Rouen, on the N154.

Although it has been repeatedly battered by war
since its foundation in the 12th century, Évreux
Cathedral retains much of interest, including
this 15th-century stained glass

Stern sentinel – Falaise Castle stands on a great bluff over the valley

FALAISE

This was the birthplace in 1027 of William the Conqueror. The massive castle, built between the 12th and 14th centuries, boasts 29 towers. Attractively rebuilt after bitter fighting in August 1944, when the Allies encircled a pocket of German resistance, an extensive restoration project finished in 1994 and a museum of the Middle Ages is planned. Climb the battlements for spectacular views and gaze out of the Chambre d'Arlette, where Duke William's father supposedly spotted the tanner's daughter at the Vieux Lavoir (see box).

Astride his charger and ready for battle, the Conqueror dominates the main square of town, which boasts a museum of automata. These mechanical figures in scenes from the 1930s and 1940s were seen originally in Parisian department store windows.

The controversial August '44 Museum features much German memorabilia.

35km south of Caen, on the N158. Château de Falaise – tel: 02 31 90 17 26. August '44 Museum – tel: 02 31 90 37 19. Open: daily April to November. Automates-Avenue. Forum – tel: 02 31 90 02 43. Open: daily April to September; weekends and holidays rest of the year. Admission charge.

GISORS

The revolutionary octagonal keep marked a breakthrough in military design back in 1097 when King William Rufus of England built it to defend the River Epte, Normandy's border with France. The castle is long gone but the keep remains atop its 20m-high hillock overlooking this pleasant small town. *57km southeast of Rouen, on the D14.*

HONFLEUR

Cafés and art galleries in stone and half-timbered buildings cluster around a small harbour where nets hang out to dry

---

THE DUKE AND THE TANNER'S DAUGHTER

Arlette, the beautiful daughter of a Falaise tanner, caught the eye of the Duke of Normandy while she was washing clothes. Some say he was standing in the 'Chambre d'Arlette' in the castle, but the plaque at the Vieux Lavoir maintains he was returning from hunting. Both versions agree that the offer was 'mistress, not marriage'. Despite that, she accepted and rode into the castle like a queen, and her son, William the Bastard, eventually became King of England.

and fishing boats putter in and out:
Honfleur is almost too good to be true.
No wonder artists like Boudin, Monet
(see page 43) and Courbet were inspired.
The nearby oil refineries of Le Havre and
the new Pont de Normandie bridge are
forgotten when you stand by La
Lieutenance, the remains of the fortified
gate and still the port offices. Here, a
plaque honours Samuel de Champlain,
founder of Québec in 1608. Up the hill,
is the Église Ste-Catherine, France's
oldest and largest wooden church, built
by shipwrights like two upside-down
boats, side-by-side. Its 18m-tall bell-
tower, the Clocher Ste-Catherine, stands
apart, on top of the former bell-ringers'
house. Off the Quai St-Étienne, the rue
de la Ville leads to the 17th-century
Greniers à Sel (salt warehouses), built
with stones from the old ramparts. The
magnificent wooden roofs once protected
10,000 tons of salt but now shelter
concerts and exhibitions.

Musée Eugène-Boudin

Compare works by Honfleur-inspired
19th-century artists such as Boudin and
Monet with contemporary local painters,

BOUDIN (1824–98)

Born in Honfleur, Eugène Boudin was
nicknamed *le roi des ciels* (the king of
the skies) by Courbet for his stirring
seascapes. But it was his constant
striving to capture light that made
him the modest precursor of the
Impressionists. The poet Baudelaire
wrote that one can guess the season,
the hour, the wind from a Boudin
painting. Honfleur honours his
memory with a museum; the Ferme
de St-Siméon, where he and the
Impressionists painted, is now a
luxury hotel.

---

then return to mundane life, with 19th-
century Norman bonnets and household
utensils.
*Rue de l'Homme-de-Bois. Tel: 02 31 89
54 00. Open: Wednesday to Monday (see
opening hours, page 22). Closed: weekday
mornings from October to mid-March.
Admission charge.*

Ferme de St-Siméon Hotel, Honfleur, where
the Impressionists had their base

Basilique Ste-Thérèse, Lisieux, completed in the 1950s

HOULGATE

Houlgate's wide sandy beach was once favoured by the very rich, but this early seaside resort has faded in recent decades. To the east, the Vaches-Noires (black cows) are actually cliffs tumbling into the sea and are a favourite haunt for fossil collectors. At low tide, covered in seaweed, they look like sleepy ruminants.

33km northeast of Caen, on the coast.

LISIEUX

A million pilgrims come each year to the 93m-high white Byzantine basilica of Ste-Thérèse, one of the biggest churches built anywhere in the world in the 20th century. Deeply pious, Thérèse Martin (born in Alençon in 1873) joined the Carmelite nunnery here at the age of 15. She died nine years later and was made a saint in 1925. At the basilica, pilgrims can see a film, attend a special mass, view the waxworks and pray to her remains in the Carmelite chapel. Her house, Les Buissonets, is on boulevard Herbet-Fournet.

Less religious visitors can enjoy the two large markets and the Cathédrale St-Pierre, an elegant example of 12th-century Gothic stonework.

51km east of Caen, on the N13.

LIVAROT

This unremarkable town gave its name to a famous and rather pungent cheese. All Livarot is now factory-made; the best uses unpasteurised milk. Buy some in the Musée du Fromage which shows how the cheese used to be made on farms.

18km southwest of Lisieux, on the D579. Musée du Fromage, 68 rue M Gambier. Tel: 02 31 63 43 13. Open: daily (see opening hours,

Ste Thérèse is responsible for turning Lisieux into a miniature Lourdes

page 22). Closed: Saturday afternoon,
Sunday, holidays; December to February.
Admission charge.

LOUVIERS

Despite damage in 1940, this town
between Rouen and Evreux retains many
charming half-timbered houses and a
church as elaborate as a small cathedral.
The River Eure splits into separate
streams which helped develop the cloth
industry between the 12th and 15th
centuries. The tourist office is in the 16th-
century home of the King's Jester.
31km southeast of Rouen, off the A13.

ORBEC

On the banks of the River Orbiquet, this
is the kind of small town that visitors tend
to by-pass because it has no famous
attraction, yet that is precisely its allure.
Window-shop and admire the appealing
old houses on the Grande Rue, where
you are allowed inside the photo-worthy,
400-year-old Vieux Manoir, the local
museum. The Église de Notre-Dame has
a vast belfry, started as a defensive tower
in the 15th century and given a more
decorative finishing touch in the 16th.
21km southeast of Lisieux, on the D519.
Vieux Manoir – tel: 02 31 32 87 15. Open:
July to September, afternoons Wednesday to
Sunday (see opening hours, page 22).

OUISTREHAM/RIVA-BELLA

Summer brings families to the wide open,
breezy beaches and promenade; the ferry
to England brings cars and returning
Britons all year round. This small resort's
claim to fame came on D-Day when the
left flank of the Allies' attack landed here.
On the coast, 14km north of Caen, on the
D514.

First for freedom: the café at Pegasus Bridge

PEGASUS BRIDGE

Named after the logo of the Parachute
Regiment that led the Allied attack on
D-Day, this bridge over the canal,
parallel to the River Orne, was a vital
target. The Pegasus Café was the first
house liberated in France and is still the
scene of emotional reunions on 6 June
each year. A commemorative museum is
planned. Sadly, the old bridge was
removed in 1993 to improve the flow of
traffic on the D514.
8km north of Caen, off the D514.

PONT-L'ÉVÊQUE

Yet another town synonymous with a
famous cheese, Pont-l'Évêque dates back
at least 700 years. It straddles three
rivers, the Calonne, Yvie and Touques.
Despite considerable damage in World
War II, there are still many fine half-
timbered houses. The courtyard of the
Aigle d'Or, the 16th-century coaching
inn at 68 rue de Vaucelles, is well worth
a look.
47km northeast of Caen, off the A13.

ST-GERMAIN-DE-LIVET, CHÂTEAU DE

Just outside Lisieux, this moated mansion demands a stop. White stone, pink brick and glazed green brick combine in an unusual and eye-catching chequerboard façade dating from the 16th century. Inside, splendid late 16th-century frescos of biblical scenes decorate the Guards' Room.

Tel: 02 31 31 00 03. Open: Wednesday to Monday (see opening hours, page 22). Closed: December and January.

ST-PIERRE-SUR-DIVES

Don't miss the enormous covered market here. After it was burnt down in 1944, restoration of the huge beams (joined only by chestnut pegs) followed original plans, so that the 900-year-old heart of the community was revived for the sale of fruit and vegetables (Mondays) and a monthly sale of antiques and bric-à-brac. A nearby bar, the Greenwich, refers to the line across the floor in the old

Antiques fair in the unmissable barn at St Pierre-sur-Dives

Benedictine abbey church; at midday, the sun shines along it through a plaque in the window. There is also a museum focusing on cheese-making techniques.
27km southeast of Caen, on the D40.

Château de Vendeuvre

This is something a little different: a collection of miniature furniture. Many pieces are inlaid with metal or ivory; some were executed as test pieces for full membership of a guild. Look for the tiny cupboard containing a craftsman's miniscule tools.

6km southwest of St-Pierre on the D271. Tel: 02 31 40 93 83. Open: daily May to September, Sunday and holidays, afternoon only rest of year. Closed: November to mid-March.

SWORD BEACH

This was the easternmost British sector of the D-Day Landings (see pages 86–9.)

THURY-HARCOURT

This rebuilt town on the River Orne is a pleasant place for relaxing. The northern gateway to the Suisse Normande (Little

Switzerland), it makes a good base for walking, canoeing on the river, riding and cycling. When tired, climb aboard the summer *Train Touristique* that meanders south to Clécy and north to Caen.

27km south of Caen, on the D562.

TROUVILLE-SUR-MER

Trouville is situated on the opposite bank of the River Touques to Deauville. Where Deauville is sophisticated, Trouville is jolly and down-to-earth, with its fishing port and quayside stalls for the catch. In fact, Trouville triggered France's sea-bathing boom 150 years ago when writers Alexandre Dumas and Gustave Flaubert sang its praises. Families stroll round the harbour and, when rain threatens, head for the Aquarium (see **Children**, page 159).

Musée Montebello

Scenes of sailors, the beach and the harbour are among paintings of 19th-century Trouville by Boudin (see page 73) and local talents. Amusing are depictions of the early days of sea-bathing, complete with pyjama-like costumes.

Rue Général Leclerc. Tel: 02 31 88 16 26. Open: April to September, afternoons Wednesday to Monday (see opening hours, page 22). Admission charge.

VERNEUIL-SUR-AVRE

Verneuil is a pretty town that is truly 'typical', with pleasant old streets (rue du Canon, rue de la Madeleine), a moat and two unusual historic remains. The 60m-tall tower of the Madeleine church recalls Rouen Cathedral's Tour de Beurre and was likewise built with the donations of penitents wanting to eat butter during Lent. The nearby Tour Grise (grey

If you like 'kiss-me-quick' resorts, you'll love Trouville-sur-Mer

tower) is a 13th-century keep built of reddish stone.

36km west of Dreux, on the N12.

VIMOUTIERS

This larger neighbour of Camembert has cashed in on the fame of that cheese. One statue of its 'inventor', Marie Harel, stands in the plain main square; another, by the church, was decapitated when the town was razed in June 1944. A small museum in the tourist office has one-legged milkstools, labels, copper churns and a multi-lingual video all about the local product.

27km south of Lisieux, on the D579. Musée du Camembert, 10 avenue Général de Gaulle. Tel: 02 33 39 30 29. Open: (see opening hours, page 22). Closed: Monday morning May to October, also Sunday, Mondy morning rest of the year.

Caen

Caen was at the centre of the D-Day attack in 1944 and was devastated by bombing and artillery fire. Miraculously, some of the medieval town survived and can be seen on this short stroll (see pages 58–63 for more details of places to see). *Allow about 45 minutes.*

Start at the Église St-Pierre, near the tourist office.

1 ÉGLISE ST-PIERRE

Although Caen's two 11th-century abbeys are more famous, this is the parish church of the city and, as such, has attracted generous gifts over the centuries. The soaring 78m-high spire built in 1317 was destroyed in 1944 but has been rebuilt. *Enter rue St-Pierre.*

2 RUE ST-PIERRE

This pedestrianised street used to have several sections, such as the *confiserie* (confectioner's) and the *mercerie* (haberdashery), named for the products sold there. Mostly post-war, it still has several medieval buildings housing high-quality shops selling chocolates, jewellery and cakes. Just after the Pavillon Christofle, peer through a gate on the left: the entry looks centuries old. Across on the right, No 54 is the Musée de la Poste (Postal Museum) in one of the finest 16th-century half-timbered houses in Caen, complete with carvings of saints. *Cross rue Notre-Dame and turn right.*

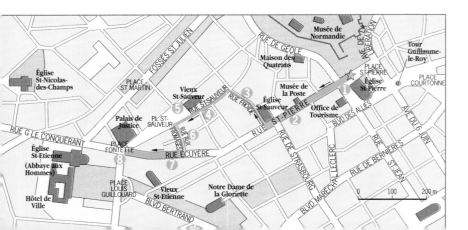

3 RUE FROIDE

The Église St-Sauveur used to be called Notre-Dame-de-Froide-Rue and is, unusually, built on a north-south axis. A plan on the left-hand wall of rue Froide shows the area in 1817. Little passages to the left and right, such as rue de la Monnaie, are atmospheric. Number 22 bis, with its grimy archway, timbered ceiling and old courtyard, has not changed in centuries. Diners at l'Amandier restaurant enjoy medieval surroundings.

At the end of rue Froide, turn left on to rue St-Sauveur.

Typical yellow-grey stone houses in Caen, an attractive town

4 RUE ST-SAUVEUR

Rooms on the upper levels of these houses still have ancient beams that are visible through the windows. Across the street looms the bulk of another St-Sauveur, Vieux St-Sauveur. Only its 12th-century tower survived the war. Restoration continues at this old butter-market church.

5 PLACE ST-SAUVEUR

Apart from being a useful car-park, this square has handsome 18th-century mansions overlooking a rather pompous statue of Louis XIV dressed as a Roman emperor. Until the last century a pillory still stood here, where the open-air market is held on Fridays.

Leave the square via the rue aux Fromages.

6 RUE AUX FROMAGES

After a few steps, the atmosphere becomes medieval thanks to cobbles and half-timbered buildings housing, appropriately, antique dealers.

Turn right into rue Ecuyere.

Oak carving on the 16th-century Musée de la Poste, rue St-Pierre

7 RUE ECUYERE

More antique dealers line this wide, pedestrianised street, an extension of rue St-Pierre. On the right, No 32 has a barred peephole; on the left, No 42, the Hôtel des Ecuyers, dates from the 15th century and was later the home of a Vicomte de Caen.

Continue to place Fontette.

8 PLACE FONTETTE

On the right is the Palais de Justice, the handsome law courts, complete with Corinthian pillars. On the far side, the bridge offers an excellent view of the Abbaye aux Hommes and the Hôtel de Ville (town hall) which took over the 18th-century monastery buildings in 1965.

APPLES AND PEARS

Say 'Normandy' and most people think of 'apples'. This fruit appears with chicken and pork, alongside *boudin* (black pudding) or stuffed into the *gâteau de Trouville* (an apple and cream cake). An apple baked in pastry is a *bourdelot* or *rabote*.

82–3). Cider is traditionally served in pottery jugs but be careful with *cidre bouché*, cider bottled with a Champagne-like cork. This sparkling version can be explosive if left in the back of a hot car.

To see how apples and pears become cider, calvados or perry, visit the museum at Barenton (below and right)

CIDER

Back in the 8th century, the Emperor Charlemagne supposedly encouraged his subjects to imbibe Normandy cider. Now demand is so great that apples have to be imported from the west of England. Labels say *doux* (sweet) or *sec/brut* (dry) and proper cider (*bon bère*) must be at least 5 per cent alcohol according to law (a weaker version has about 3.5 per cent alcohol). Even without fluent French, it's fun to stop for a *dégustation* (tasting) at farms that produce the brew. Around Cambremer, southeast of Caen, signs proclaim *Cru de Cambremer* (grown in Cambremer, vintage Cambremer) which locals boast is the best (see pages

CALVADOS

Distil cider and you get calvados. The Normans learned how 400 years ago from their neighbours on the Loire, but it was only in the 19th century that standards were set at today's high level. Strict rules must be followed to receive the AOC (*Appellation d'Origine Contrôlée*) stamp of approval. By

adding a little yeast, the mashed-up apples are fermented; the resulting liquid is distilled twice, often in glowing copper alembics. After maturation in oak casks for five to 10 years, special committees taste it before certificating it for sale. Some calvados is aged for 30 years in white bottles labelled *Hors d'Âge* (ageless) and connoisseurs rate the best an equal to the finest cognac.

THE NORMAN HOLE

The legendary *trou Normand*, a shot of 'calva' drunk part way through a meal, drills a hole to make way for more food. Nowadays, a calvados-flavoured sorbet serves the purpose in some restaurants.

POMMEAU

This chilled cocktail is two parts apple *moût* (must, juice), one part calvados. Beware: it slips down all too easily, but packs a punch.

THE PEAR

A pear baked in pastry is a *douillon*, and around Domfront the small, hard fruit is crushed and mashed like apples for a fruity, sparkling *poiré* (perry).

Cider Country

Normandy's small lanes are excellent for cyclists, although the lack of sign posts can be a hazard, particularly if you stop for *dégustations* (tastings). This route follows part of the well-marked Route du Cidre (cider trail) through the lovely Auge Valley (17km). The best producers are indicated by the Cru de Cambremer signs.

Allow 2 to 3 hours.

Start in Cambremer.

1 CAMBREMER

This village has a small information centre on the place de l'Église, with its pretty parish church topped by a surprisingly

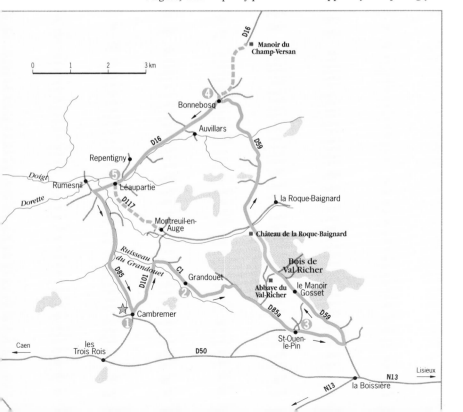

large 11th-century tower. The *Cru de Cambremer* cider festival is celebrated on 15 May each year, while the old-fashioned market is on Sunday mornings in July and August plus Easter, and the two national holidays in May.

Take the D101 signed la Roque-Baignard, following Route du Cidre sign. Cross the Ruisseau du Grandouet. Turn right on to the C1 for 1km to Grandouet.

2 GRANDOUET

This hamlet has a charming small church as well as M Giard's farm where he makes cider.

Continue up the hill, rejoining the D85a. Turn right. Pedal past fields and woods. At a T-junction, turn left towards la Boissière and enter St-Ouen-le-Pin.

3 ST-OUEN-LE-PIN

André Gide, who won the Nobel prize for literature in 1947, was mayor of this straggling village in his younger days. The 19th-century diplomat François Guizot, author of histories of the English Revolution and of European civilisation, is buried here.

At the crossroads, turn left on the D59 to Bonnebosq and re-enter St-Ouen-le-Pin. In a small, modern house on the right, another cider-maker, Michel Lesufleur, offers dégustations. The road to Bonnebosq is a pretty run past a stream and pond. Look left for the 17th-century Abbaye du Val-Richer (Abbey of Val Richer) where Guizot lived his later years (not open to the public). Another splendid private residence on the left, complete with moat, is the Château de la Roque-Baignard.

4 BONNEBOSQ

If there is time, the peaceful little-visited 16th-century Manoir du Champ-Versan, a few minutes along the D16, is worth a

Even if you don't particularly like cider you will enjoy cycling this route – but try to go when the blossom is out

detour to see the huge fireplaces (tel: 02 31 65 11 07; open: afternoons daily, Easter to October; closed Monday, Tuesday, also Monday in July and August).

On leaving Bonnebosq, turn off the Route du Cidre and left almost immediately on to the D16 to Léaupartie.

5 LÉAUPARTIE

Locals boast that their Mairie is the smallest in France but they are also proud of the famous stud. Energetic cyclists can take a detour on the D117 to Montreuil-en-Auge. A few minutes away is the Vieille Auberge. This century-old inn is popular with cyclists, who stop for refreshment and relaxation while exploring the little lanes and tasting home-produced cider.

Back in Léaupartie, turn left on to the D85 to Cambremer. Cycle through orchards that are full of blossom in spring. In autumn, hessian sacks stand bulging with apples. As you re-enter Cambremer, on the left, M Forcher is another well-known cider producer. Return to the church.

Cheese Country

Normandy's fame for cheese depends on its rich pastures. This drive through the Pays d'Auge follows narrow lanes through cosy valleys and past small fields bordered by hedges. It also takes in tiny villages and historic relics. *Allow 2 hours.*

Start in Vimoutiers.

1 VIMOUTIERS

The Camembert museum (in the tourist office) is an appropriate starting point. Drive up the hill towards the church. Beside the road is the statue of Marie Harel (inventor of Camembert, see page 69). Erected in 1928, it was decapitated in World War II bombing.
Turn left on the D916 then bear left on the D16 towards Camembert. At the bottom of the hill, turn right on the D246 to Camembert, past wayside farms advertising home-made cheese. A

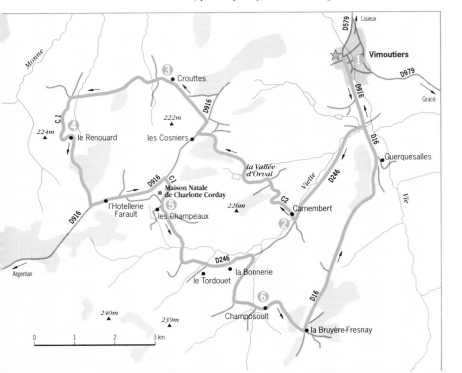

huge cross on the left stands opposite a stone stele dedicated to Marie Harel. Take this right turn across a bridge and up the hill.

2 CAMEMBERT

In this hamlet, the modern Maison du Camembert faces the 16th-century manor house of Beaumoncel where the legendary recipe was handed on.

Continue over the hill on the C2, a single-track road. Halfway down, bear left at a T-junction into the valley of the River Orval. At the main road, the D916, turn right, back towards Vimoutiers. Turn left soon, next to a small modern cottage on an unmarked side road to Crouttes.

3 CROUTTES

It is easy to spot the spire of the church where Marie Harel was baptised in 1761. The Prieuré St-Michel beyond, with its 13th-century chapel and granary, is now a centre for arts and crafts (tel: 02 33 39 15 15; open afternoons daily May to September; free).

Leave Crouttes. Half-way up the hill, turn left on to the C1 for le Renouard, going up a lane marked 'Église'. (If you reach the brick schoolhouse and Mairie, you've gone too far.)

4 LE RENOUARD

Look across the valley to the church of le Renouard and a remarkable fortified manor-house with restored stone tower, arches and half-timbering. Past the church, the road wriggles through woods.

Back at the D916, turn left towards Vimoutiers. Take the abrupt right on to the C1 to les Champeaux and Maison Natale de Charlotte Corday.

A cheesemaker and his cheese. Michael Touzé of le Bôquet Farm, Vieux Pont

5 MAISON NATALE DE CHARLOTTE CORDAY

The young noblewoman, Charlotte Corday, is remembered for stabbing Jacobin politician Marat in his bath in 1793. A descendant of the 17th-century playwright Corneille, Corday was born in this small Norman farmhouse (on the left, not open to the public) on 27 July, 1768.

Continue past the Église des Lignerits, the church where Corday was baptised. Turn left at the T-junction, and left again on to the D246. At le Tordouet, Michel Delorme still produces Camembert in the traditional way (tel: 02 33 39 12 56; visits by appointment). There are also several fine stud farms here. Just after the Haras de la Bonnerie, turn sharply right towards Champosoult. The road passes Domaine Hectot, producer of a renowned Camembert (not open to the public).

6 CHAMPOSOULT

Champosoult is where Marie Harel lived and died. The old house is not open to the public; her tomb is in the graveyard.

Continue to la Bruyère-Fresnay, whose modern church contrasts with the ancient Norman style. Then rejoin the main road, the D16, and return to Vimoutiers.

The D-Day Beaches

This 140km route, from the mouth of the River Orne to the neck of the Cotentin Peninsula, follows the D-Day beaches past monuments and museums honouring the invasion forces. *Allow at least half a day, more with stops.*

Leave Caen on the D515 for Ouistreham. Turn off on the D141 to Bénouville and Pegasus Bridge.

1 PEGASUS BRIDGE

The eastern flank of the invasion is named for the emblem of the British 5th Parachute Brigade: this bridge and café were the first to be liberated in the early hours of 6 June, 1944. Too narrow for traffic, the old iron bridge was removed in 1993.
Return to the D515 for Ouistreham. Follow the Circuit du Débarquement signs.

2 OUISTREHAM/RIVA-BELLA

A grim blockhouse, part of Germany's 'Atlantic Wall', survives one block inland. A small Commando museum across from the casino and a memorial in nearby dunes commemorate the first French troops to return to their native soil.
Follow the D514 through resorts with streets named for D-Day heroes and tanks in main squares. Langrune is the border between Sword and Juno Beaches. In St-Aubin and Bernières, memorials to

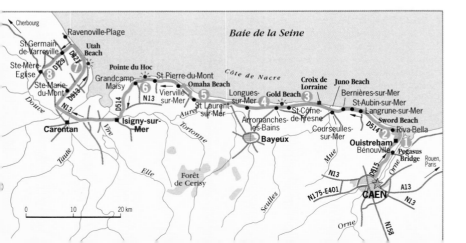

Men of the RAF Signals Unit laying tracks over quicksand

the Canadian forces stand alongside neat white bathing huts.

3 COURSEULLES-SUR-MER

Fishing boats bob beneath a gigantic cross of Lorraine, where General de Gaulle, leader of the Free French, triumphantly returned on 14 June. This is the end of Juno and the beginning of Gold Beach. *Continue on the D514 past St-Côme-de-Fresne where, high on the cliffs, an orientation platform shows who came from where on D-Day.*

4 ARROMANCHES-LES-BAINS

Remnants of a Mulberry harbour, floated from England, are still visible offshore; the museum tells the story (see page 97). *Follow the D514 to Longues, where the German battery remains, and through Port-en-Bessin, whose museum features shipwrecks hoisted from the deep. On the D514, follow the sign to Omaha Beach, turning right on to the single track road.*

5 OMAHA BEACH

A wooden stile guards the rose-bordered path leading to a fortified point. The main concentration of American troops landed below. *The lane leads to a vast American cemetery with rows of white crosses. Return to the D514, passing Vierville with its three-sided*

memorial to the US National Guard. At Criqueville-en-Bessin, turn right to Pointe du Hoc.

6 POINTE DU HOC

Bleak and grim, the force of attack and defence is still felt here, thanks to craters, semi-ruined bunkers and twisted steel wire. The US Rangers suffered horrific losses storming these crumbling brown cliffs. *Return to the D514. Turn right towards Grandcamp-Maisy with its Ranger Museum. Join the N13 towards Cherbourg; exit on the D913 for Ste-Marie-du-Mont, where signs in the village recount local events on D-Day. Continue to Utah Beach.*

7 UTAH BEACH

A pink bollard marked '00' is the first kilometre-marker on la Voie de la Liberté, the road to European liberty. *Take the D421 towards Ravenoville-Plage. Watch for the D129 on the left; turn on to Davis Road, one of many named for non-commissioned soldiers who died here on D-Day. Take this to Ste-Mère-Église via St-Germain-de-Varreville.*

8 STE-MÈRE-ÉGLISE

The western flank of the D-Day landing was secured by US paratroops. Visit the excellent museum (see page 106).

D-DAY

It takes only a matter of minutes to drive the 14km from Ouistreham to Caen; in 1944, it took Allied troops 34 days to fight their way from the beaches to the city. Moreover, the ferocity of the fighting after D-Day and the length of the Battle of Normandy are often forgotten in the blaze of military glory surrounding what was code-named 'Operation Overlord'.

The Allies worked hard to fool the Germans into believing that the invasion would attack the Pas de Calais across the narrow neck of the English Channel. Instead, it was directed at the 80km-wide stretch of Normandy coast between the Caen Canal in the east and the base of the Cotentin Peninsula in the west. In the early hours of 6 June, 135,000 troops and 20,000 vehicles landed on five sections, or beaches: Sword, Juno, Gold (British and Canadian forces) and Omaha and Utah (US forces) between 6.30 and 7.30am.

Earlier, just after midnight, paratroopers dropped to secure the eastern and western flanks. The 4,000 ships covered by 5,800 bombers and 4,900 fighters, constituted the greatest invasion force in history: the German Seventh Army, with its six Panzer divisions and 36 infantry divisions, was taken by surprise.

Nevertheless, the invasion was not easy; despite mine-removal tanks for the infantry there were

Top: landing on 6 June
Above: one of the many memorials
Left: Liberty Way marker

11,000 casualties including 2,500 dead on 6 June. The American 1st Division had a desperate struggle to capture Omaha Beach, overlooked by the massive defences on the elevated Pointe du Hoc.

Back-up support was vital; fresh troops, vehicles and ammunition ferried across in the invasion's wake used the unique,

Top: Sherman tank at Courseulles, Juno Beach
Centre: Sword Beach today
Above: anti-aircraft gun in action, 8 June

floating Mulberry harbour, towed across the Channel to Arromanches. German reinforcements held up the advance and it was three weeks before Cherbourg and the Cotentin Peninsula were taken. The first 48 days' fighting cost 117,000 German casualties, the Allies a further 122,000, but Hitler's refusal to retreat played into the Allies' hands; the Germans were trapped in a pincer move in the Falaise Pocket and by 21 August the Battle of Normandy was over. Paris was liberated on 25 August, 1944.

Western Normandy

*T*his region boasts two of the best known sights in France: Mont-St-Michel and the Bayeux Tapestry. One is a triumph of grand-scale engineering, the other a masterpiece of the minute: both attract visitors from all over the world. Then there are the beaches of D-Day, 6 June, 1944. The older generation come to remember and pay their respects to fallen comrades, the younger to learn just how dangerous and difficult the Allied invasion actually was.

From Ouistreham (in Central Normandy) to Ste-Mère-Église, via Courseulles, Arromanches and Utah Beach the coast is fringed with unattractive modern cottages and hotels. Mainly flat and open, these beaches would hold little attraction were it not

for this famous moment in history.

The upthrust of the Contentin peninsula presents a different Normandy: tall, dark cliffs, grey stone villages and a sense of remoteness. Cherbourg, dominated by a hilltop fortress, is undergoing a face-lift to pretty up its rugged image as a naval base. Bollards along the Voie de la Liberté mark the 1,145km Liberty Road (from the Cotentin to Bastogne in Belgium) beginning with '0' at Ste-Mère-Église and '00' at Utah Beach.

The west coast of the peninsula is dramatic (see pages 110–11) but there are also seaside resorts like Barneville-Carteret and Granville where families can swim in the clean, if cold, waters straight from the Atlantic.

Inland, the countryside is full of the unexpected. Coutances and Avranches have imposing churches that seem overlarge for these towns, while in Valognes, the market square and 18th-century mansions are surprisingly grand. Lessay's annual fair brings some 250,000 visitors to look at domestic livestock.

Villedieu-les-Poêles has a tradition of metalwork, from copper *poêles* (frying pans) to pewter and even bells, still cast at a cobwebbed foundry. Some souvenirs may have a tacky shine but don't be put

One of those silhouettes that everyone is familiar with: Mont-St-Michel off: there is high-quality cookware on offer, too. Similarly, imports from elsewhere often overshadow the well-made, traditional pottery of Noron-la-Poterie near Bayeux.

Here and there are abbeys that have succumbed to time and the French Revolution. Cérisy has lost most of its nave though long stretches of back-breakingly-built stone walls still edge the monastery's land. White-painted fences, on the other hand, signpost stud farms and the haras at St-Lô is one of France's best-known national studs.

WESTERN NORMANDY

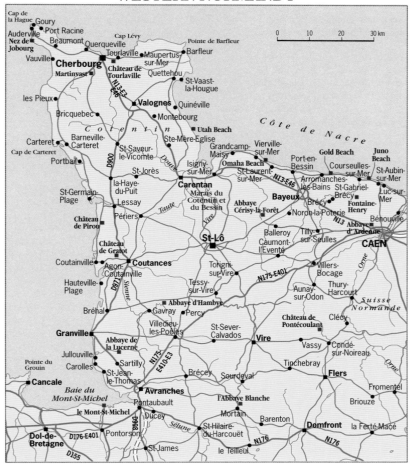

Bayeux

'We've seen the tapestry, so what else is there?' Bayeux has worked hard in recent years to live up to the fame of 'the Conquest Hanging', as it used to be called. First came the Centre Guillaume le Conquérant to properly display and explain La Tapisserie, then the new Musée Mémorial de la Bataille de Normandie 1944. The town itself, with cobbled streets and historic houses escaped serious damage in the post-D-Day fighting, thanks to Dom Aubourg, a chaplain at St-Vigor's Priory. Having convinced the Allied troops that the Germans had fled, his reward was seeing the *tricolore* raised on 7 June over the first liberated city in France.

There is more to its history, however, than 1066 and 1944. In 905, Bayeux became the 'cradle of the Norman Empire' when a son was born to the daughter of the governor and the Viking leader, Rollo, later first Duke of Normandy. Unfortunately, William the

The central tower of Bayeux Cathedral, with its 19th-century copper 'bonnet'

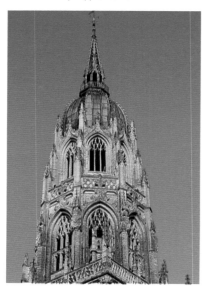

Conqueror had no sentimental feeling and sacked the town while suppressing rebellious barons; later, its cathedral was built by his half-brother, Bishop Odo, with profits from the invasion of England.

In the Middle Ages, neighbouring Caen grew in power and Bayeux became a backwater. Lahaeudrie, a 19th-century historian, wrote that '... the town remains ... veiled in an atmosphere of soothing melancholy mingled with a powerful feeling of the past.'

That sense of history is today's great attraction. Street names still read like a shopping directory: rue Laitière (for buying milk), rue de la Poissonnerie (the fishmarket) and rue des Cuisiniers (the cooks). Rue Franche, however, was named by St-Manvieu; having brought an infant back to life as it was about to be buried, the saint ordered that no one doomed to die should use Franche, or Free Street.

The town's oldest house, a classic of medieval half-timbering (formerly the tourist office) is on rue St-Martin opposite the 18th-century Maison du Cadran, decorated with a sundial and a 'month' dial. Look along the tiny side streets towards the cathedral for glimpses of its tower and spires; admire the 18th-century *hôtels* (town mansions) built of pale stone behind elaborate gates. The centre of Bayeux is small but full of charm.

Cathédrale Notre-Dame
The Bayeux Tapestry was displayed on special days in the cathedral, where 'improvements' over the centuries include the copper 'bonnet' on the lantern tower, dating from the 19th century. Yet the look is essentially Norman: over 100m long and 22m high, with rounded arches decorated with Scandinavian and Anglo-Saxon designs. Spot the monsters and monkeys cavorting in the carved 'basketwork' pattern.
Place des Tribunaux.

View along the length of the cathedral nave during Sunday morning mass

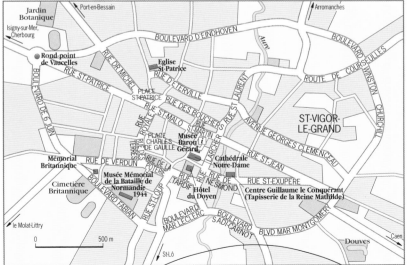

BAYEUX

Tapisserie de Bayeux (Bayeux Tapestry)

'Item, a very long piece of cloth embroidered with pictures and inscriptions representing the conquest of England ...' That listing in the 1476 inventory of Bayeux Cathedral refers to one of the most famous pieces of sewing in the world. As simple as a strip cartoon, it portrays the events leading up to and including the Battle of Hastings, where William of Normandy defeated King Harold of England. Legend has it that Queen Matilda and her ladies-in-waiting stitched the embroidery. Historians surmise that monks produced it by sewing wool on linen on the orders of Odo, Bishop of Bayeux, William's half-brother. The tapestry would have been exhibited for the first time when Bayeux cathedral was dedicated in 1077, in William's

Tapestry detail: King Harold (centre) is shot through the eye with an arrow

presence. But is this an historical record or 11th-century Norman propaganda? Work your way through the various exhibitions, listen to the headset, study the tapestry, and then decide for yourself.

Salle Guillaume

With music and slides, projected on to a fleet of white 'sails', the story of the Danish invasions of western Europe is told. An exhibition expands the story of the tapestry and shows how William stamped his authority on England after 1066.

Salle Mathilde

Maps place the to-ings and fro-ings across the English Channel into context and an excellent 14-minute film (alternate showings in French and English) tells the tale of William's life, unravels the political machinations leading to the invasion and focuses on the tapestry in detail.

Tapestry detail: loading the fleet with provisions for the invasion

The Tapestry

It is not a series of huge wall hangings but a long, narrow cloth (70m by 0.5m) with 'almost juvenile stitching' in rust red, moss green and slate blue. Some panels show static figures, others have plenty of action, with horses trotting and pulling on the reins. Look in the borders for rude drawings and grotesque animals, the needlework equivalent of gargoyles. Of the 58 panels, these are some of the key scenes.

Panel 23: Harold swears the oath of allegiance to William, touching the Gospels and a holy relic. This is the basis of William's claim to the English throne.

Panel 26: The body of King Edward the Confessor is carried to Westminster Abbey. Note the two small figures with funeral bells; also, the hand of God stretching down from heaven.

Panels 32 and 33: Harold has been crowned king but a comet foretells doom. In the lower border, five boats predict the invasion of England.

Panels 37 and 38: Crossing the English Channel: first, casks of wine, suits of chain mail, swords and axes are loaded; then a stiff wind catches the sails; finally, the horses are led off and the boats pulled up on shore.

Panels 42 and 43: Note the spit-roasted chickens and kebabs, served up at a banquet.

Panels 40 and 47: Separated by the feast, these panels show the invaders stealing sheep, cattle and plate, then setting fire to a house, leaving a mother and child homeless.

Panel 48: Mounted soldiers in silver-thread chain mail charge into battle, lances at the ready. William and his half-brother, Bishop Odo, however, carry maces.

The following scenes are full of detail, from delicately stitched arrows to the horror of upended horses, decapitated bodies and hand-to-hand combat.

Panel 55: Rumour has it that William is dead; lifting his visor, he rallies his troops before the final assault.

Panel 57: A golden arrow pierces Harold's eye and skull, killing him. After 14 hours, the battle is over. On 14 October, 1066, William of Normandy is King of England.

Centre Guillaume le Conquérant, rue de Nesmond. Tel: 02 31 51 25 50. Open: daily. Admission charge; a special ticket covers this plus the three smaller museums in Bayeux.

Musée Baron Gérard

This fine, small museum's eclectic collection ranges from old pharmacy bottles to a 17th-century cabinet that is a *tour de force* of marquetry. Most interesting are displays of local porcelain, pottery and lace. Apple blossom and forget-me-nots decorate 19th-century Bayeux porcelain, whose slight blue tinge typifies china clay from the Manche. Salt glaze, on the other hand, produces the bluish lustre of the pottery (see box on page 104), still made in nearby Noron-la-Poterie. Examples of local lace justify its renown, especially the black, with a shadow effect, and the '*blonde*' (ivory silk). In Bayeux, *fuseaux* (spindles) were used; note the personalised set from 1840: '*je suis de Victorine*'.
Place de la Liberté. Tel: 02 31 92 14 21. Open: daily (see opening hours, page 22). Admission charge.

Musée Diocésain d'Art Religieux and Conservatoire de la Dentelle de Bayeux

The lace-making school is fascinating. Here women carry on the town's proud tradition in the Hôtel du Doyen. By comparison, the collection of religious art is dull.
Rue Lambert-Leforestier. Tel: 02 31 92 14 21/31 92 73 80. Open: daily (see opening hours, page 22). Admission charge.

Musée Mémorial de la Bataille de Normandie 1944

This museum, tracing the 76-day Battle of Normandy, is one of the best of its kind. Covering the build-up as well as the action, the foot soldiers as well as the major players, the museum appeals to children as well as to veterans. Newspapers of the day are juxtaposed with propaganda leaflets; a 'letter to Mom' is next to a Purple Heart, the American military medal. A diorama, complete with rubble, shows Poles and Americans meeting up on 19 August, 1944, and a film (French and English) tells the story, with original footage.
Boulevard Fabian Ware. Tel: 02 31 92 93 41. Open: daily (see opening hours, page 22). Admission charge.

ARROMANCHES-LES-BAINS

A Mulberry Harbour, made in England and floated across the Channel, allowed

Inside the Château de Balleroy, built by François Mansart

2½ million soldiers, half a million vehicles and 4 million tons of equipment to land in the 100 days after D-Day. At low tide, remnants of the half-million tons of concrete linked by 16km of steel 'roads' are visible. Arromanches 360 is an 18-minute film which re-creates the event (tel: 02 31 22 30 30; admission charge).

Musée du Débarquement
Dioramas, models, films and photographs recall the historic dawn of 6 June, 1944. *Tel: 02 31 22 34 31. Open: daily (see opening hours, page 22). Closed: January. Admission charge.*

Arromanches is on the coast, 31km northwest of Caen.

AVRANCHES
In the 8th century, St Aubert, Bishop of Avranches, foolishly disregarded two visions of St Michael ordering him to build a chapel. The third time, the archangel poked his *doigt de feu* (fiery finger) in the bishop's skull ... and Mont-St-Michel was then built. There are splendid views of it from the Jardin des Plantes, while the bishop's perforated

Arromanches-les-Bains, with the remains of the Mulberry Harbour

pate is in the treasury of the Basilica of St Gervais. Illuminated manuscripts from Mont-St-Michel are displayed in summer in the Town Hall.

At the west end of the Bishop's Palace is the Square Thomas à Becket where a stone tablet marks the spot where King Henry II of England did penance and received papal absolution in 1172 for involvement in the murder of Thomas à Becket. The place Patton commemorates General Patton's 1944 success against the German counter-attack from the Mortain pocket. *100km southwest of Caen, off the N175.*

BALLEROY, CHÂTEAU DE
This haughty 17th-century pink and grey mansion stares down its avenue straight into the village. In the Waterloo Room, portraits of Napoleon and the Duke of Wellington glower at one another across the fireplace. It is owned by the family of the late Malcolm Forbes, the American magazine publisher. A balloon enthusiast, his museum portrays ballooning from Montgolfier in 1783 to the barrage balloons of World War II. *15km southwest of Bayeux, off the D572. Tel: 31 21 60 61. Open: daily Easter to mid-October. Closed: Wednesday. Admission charge.*

BARENTON

The Maison de la Pomme et de la Poire tells the story of cider and calvados as well as of the varieties of apples and pears in the orchards surrounding this old farm.

10km southeast of Mortain, on the D907. Tel: 02 33 59 56 22. Open: daily April to end-September (see opening hours, page 22). Admission charge.

BARFLEUR

A charming harbour full of fishing boats faced by granite cottages with stone roofs, Barfleur has its fair share of sailors' tales: William the Conqueror's boat the *Mora* was built here; later, in 1120, the *Blanche Nef* (White Ship) sank in the fierce offshore currents with 300 noblemen and King Henry I of

Mussel picker at Barfleur, with the light-house in the distance

England's only son, William, aboard. In 1194, King Richard the Lionheart sailed back to England after his release from captivity in Austria. Barfleur claims France's first lifeboat station (1865) and one of the tallest lighthouses. Climb one

step for each day of the year to reach the fabulous view, 74.85m up.

27km east of Cherbourg, on the D901. Phare de Gatteville, 5km north of Barfleur (D116 then D10). Tel: 02 35 54 04 46. Open: daily, weather and duties permitting. Free.

Plaque in Barfleur showing William's ship, the *Mora*, but did the Conqueror sail from here?

BARNEVILLE-CARTERET

Since 1965, three villages have become one: Carteret, a commercial harbour; Barneville, the old inland village; and Barneville-Plage, the newer resort and marina. The rocky Cap de Carteret protects a curving bay which has a sandy nature reserve set on dunes on the far side of the Gerfleur estuary. Legend says that the Channel Islands were separated from mainland France in 709 by a tidal wave. This is one of the most popular family resorts on the Cotentin peninsula.

On the coast, 38km southwest of Cherbourg, via the D904.

CÉRISY-LA-FORÊT, ABBAYE

The main road from Bayeux to St-Lô cuts through the beech forest of Cérisy; turn off for this Benedictine abbey which would have been awesome 800 years ago. Now, even though a large slice of its nave is missing, it is imposing, with three tiers of windows in the chancel plus a square tower and spire soaring above the 15th-century choir stalls.

Tel: 02 33 57 34 63. Open: daily Easter to mid-November. Free.

CHERBOURG

Over a million ferry passengers a year stream through this port; now Cherbourg

Fishing boats on Quai Alexandre III, Cherbourg

is sprucing up its image, hoping to tempt them to linger. A new *gare maritime* (ferry terminal) has been built; the Chantereyne marina has opened near the French navy's nuclear submarine base; and the former fish market has been replaced by a smart indoor market and leisure centre. Trees have been planted along quaysides, cafés spill on to pavements and old houses are being renovated. The 1963 film, *Les Parapluies de Cherbourg* (The Umbrellas of Cherbourg) was re-released in 1992, tempting a new generation of Catherine Deneuve fans to seek out the umbrella shop in the rue du Port.

Musée Thomas-Henry
This art collection includes works by native son Jean-François Millet, born in 1814 at Gruchy, west of Cherbourg. *Centre Culturel, rue Vastel. Tel: 02 33 23 02 23. Open: Tuesday to Sunday (see opening hours, page 22). Admission charge.*

Musée de la Libération
The Fort du Roule, 112m above Cherbourg, looks out across the *digues* (breakwaters) planned in the 17th century but not completed for 200 years. More 'experience' than museum, since its revamping in 1994, it contrasts the bleakness of the Occupation years with the relief of Liberation. Take the shuttle bus up from the bottom of the hill. *Tel: 02 33 20 14 12. Open: daily (see opening hours, page 22). Closed: Monday in winter. Admission charge.*

COURSEULLES-SUR-MER
Courseulles is a small, unsophisticated seaside resort with a broad beach, good oysters and one of the best aquariums in Normandy, La Maison de la Mer. After D-Day, its sheltered harbour welcomed Winston Churchill (12 June) and General de Gaulle (14 June). A huge cross of Lorraine (symbol of the free French) marks the spot. Over the River Seulles, however, is Graye, which also has a cross (in the dunes) and also claims the honour of 'de Gaulle's first footsteps back on French soil'. *On the coast, 18km northeast of Caen, on the D514. Maison de la Mer, place du 6 Juin. Tel: 02 31 37 92 58. Open: daily (see opening hours, page 22). Closed: Monday from October to April. Admission charge.*

Château Fontaine-Henry, with the earliest part of the building on the right

COUTANCES

The administrative and religious centre of the Cotentin Peninsula is built on a hill, with the Cathedral of Notre-Dame at the very top. After a fire in 1218, the foundations, towers and nave of the original church were cleverly incorporated into the reconstruction. The result is notable for its twin spires and 'Le Plomb'. This 40m-high lantern tower illuminates the altar below and was dubbed 'the work of a sublime madman' by 17th-century military engineer, Sébastien Vauban. Join one of the free guided tours (daily in summer, weekends in winter) to fully appreciate what Victor Hugo considered second only to Chartres in beauty.

75km south of Cherbourg, on the D2.

FONTAINE-HENRY, CHÂTEAU

Start with a small fort on the River Mue; build two wings between 1490 and 1550; the result: a lesson in architecture. Looking from right to left, you see first, the basic, fortified house, then the 'artistic' middle wing with its three-storey square tower decorated with friezes and pilasters. Finally, there is the extraordinary, wedge-shaped slate roof, steep as a mountain-side. More or less the same family has lived here for five centuries and their collection of paintings and antiques is on view to the public.

12km northwest of Caen, off the D22. Tel: 02 31 80 00 42. Open: weekend afternoons Easter to early November; afternoons daily mid-June to mid-September. Admission charge.

GOLD BEACH

The westernmost of the three British sectors on D-Day (see pages 86–9).

GRANVILLE

Before it became a leisure and pleasure destination in the mid-19th century, the

Sumptuous bedroom in Château Fontaine-Henry

Rooftop view over Granville's houses

value of this rocky promontory was strategic. Indeed, the military are still based behind the ramparts of the Haute Ville (Upper Town), which withstood a siege in the upheaval after the Revolution. A plaque at the Grand Porte recalls the struggle. Below the drawbridge are narrow streets; below them, the harbour and beaches. To the south are marinas; to the north, the casino. Take a solitary walk to the tip of the promontory or join in the many family and seaside entertainments.

Aquarium du Roc

Fish, model ships plus shells, minerals and a butterfly garden.
Tel: 02 33 50 19 10. Open: daily Palm Sunday to mid-September.

Christian Dior Museum

The fashion designer grew up in this elegant cliff-top house with its fine gardens. Rotating exhibitions.
Tel: 02 33 61 48 21. Open: daily April to October. Admission charge.

Îles Chausey

Just 15km offshore, these granite rocks

were quarried for Mont-St-Michel and the pavements of Paris and London. The ferocious tide – one of the biggest in the world – rises and falls some 14m. Grande Île (2km long) is large enough for a small hotel, a fort and a lighthouse. Day trips from Granville take 50 minutes each way to visit the '52 islets and 365 rocks'.

Granville is on the coast, 105km south of Cherbourg, off the D971.

HAMBYE, ABBAYE D'

With towering walls but no roof, this ruined 13th-century abbey is imposing yet peaceful, guarded by a steep, wooded escarpment. Though off the beaten track, it is worth the detour up the Sienne Valley for romantics and abbey-enthusiasts. There is also a small library of religious vestments and tapestries.
3km south of Hambye, on the D51. Tel: 02 33 61 76 92. Open: daily, May to mid-October. Closed: Tuesday. Admission charge.

JUNO BEACH

The middle of the three-pronged British attack on D-Day (see pages 86–9).

Mont-St-Michel

Some 150m above the waves, the gilded statue of the Archangel Michael glistens atop the 100-year-old spire: Mont-St-Michel is a familiar sight from countless postcards and posters. From a distance, the buildings look like outcrops of the rock itself; then the eye picks out half-timbered houses, stone walls, green gardens and the fortress-abbey at the top. A seven-year plan will confine traffic to the mainland and restore the Mount's isolation – eventually.

To avoid the crowds, visit out of season or midweek. Arrive early in the morning or stay the night in one of the 140 hotel rooms so you can wander along cobbled streets in peace. Or, like pilgrims of old, walk from Genêts across the sands with a

guide (two hours each way, 12km in all). *Maison de la Baie du Mont-St-Michel, place de la Mairie, Genêts. Tel: 02 33 70 86 46.*

Porte du Roy (King's Gate)

Two *michelettes* (huge mortars) are reminders of English attacks during the Hundred Years' War. Cross the drawbridge, pass under the portcullis and through the iron gate; to the left is one of the world's best-known restaurants, opened by Mère Poulard a century ago and still serving fluffy omelettes her way, cooked over wood fires. The Grande Rue, just a narrow lane, curves uphill between shops, cafés and restaurants. To avoid the human traffic jams, make for the ramparts and follow the path up to rejoin the main approach to the Grand Degré staircase.

The abbey and its church

Pity the novice lost in the corridors, chapels and stairways of this enormous complex. From the Terrasse de l'Ouest (Western Terrace), the panorama stretches across to Brittany. Inside the Sacristy, four simple models show how the mount was built: on three levels, with the lower two supporting the top platform

Buildings have been added, rebuilt and adapted on Mont-St-Michel for more than 1,000 years

with its cloisters, refectory and church, where the present community of three monks and two nuns attend mass. Over 800 years old, its soaring, barrel-vaulted ceiling is wooden, like that of the cloisters, where a modern picture-window looks straight down to the sea. In the echoing dining-room, the windows are cleverly angled to project the voice of the monk reading from the Bible during meals.

Discover your own favourite spots: perhaps the carving of the Bishop of Avranches being 'persuaded' to build the first church (see page 97), or the huge wooden wheel turned by prisoners' leg-power to haul up supplies from below when this was a gaol after the French Revolution.

Between June and September, Les Imaginaires, an intriguing late-night mixture of music and light brings the ancient buildings to life (see page 152). *Tel: 02 33 89 80 00. Open: daily. Admission charge.*

Wax bishop outside the Musée Historique

Constable of France, Bertrand du Guesclin and his wife, Tiphaine. *Tel: 02 33 60 23 34. Open: daily mid-February to mid-November. Closed: Friday. Admission charge.*

Archéoscope

Here, legends about the Mount are recounted in hi-tech visuals. *Tel: 02 33 48 09 37. Open: daily, February to mid-November (see opening hours, page 22). Admission charge (one ticket covers this, the Musée Grévin and the Musée Maritime).*

Logis Tiphaine

Tapestries and furniture, including a finely-carved marriage wardrobe, evoke days gone by in this house, built in 1365 by the

Musée Historique

This tells the story of the Mount in dioramas highlighted by light and sound. Children demand a look through the periscope for views of the bay. *Tel: 02 33 60 14 09.*

Musée Maritime

An explanation of the phenomenon of tides plus 250 models of boats makes this a useful attraction for families. *As above.*

Buy your souvenirs in the Mont's Grand Rue

MORTAIN

In the old days this outpost defended southern Normandy from Maine and Brittany; in 1944 it was crucial to Hitler's personally-planned counter-attack after the D-Day invasion. In town, the church of St Evroult has an 11th-century doorway decorated with a carved sawtooth pattern. Inside, a 7th-century Anglo-Irish _Chrismale_ (wooden coffer lined with copper) bears runic inscriptions; legend maintains that it is the Holy Grail. Indiana Jones has yet to visit.

Largely rebuilt in the 1950s, this hillside town is a good base for exploring the countryside. Two waterfalls, the 24m Grande Cascade on the River Cance and the Petite Cascade on the River Cançon, are pretty rather than impressive, but make a nice walk on a fine afternoon. Just across the road is the Abbaye Blanche, founded in the 12th century. Named for the _dames blanches_ (white ladies) of the Cistercian order, it is now occupied by monks.
63km south of St-Lô, on the D977. Abbaye Blanche. Tel: 02 33 59 00 21. Open: Wednesday to Monday (closed Sunday

> ### SALT-GLAZE POTTERY
> Noron pottery was part of everyday life in the region. Workers took a _bonbonne_, a 5-litre jug of cider to the fields; the classic _cruchon_, a small jug with handle and stopper, held calvados ... and still does in many households. The dairy industry used tall, cylindrical _machons_ for exporting butter while coffee is still served in _cannes_ (pitchers). The dark brown pottery made from local red clay is sprayed with fine salt during baking to produce a bluish lustre. Random sprinkling gives an attractive irregularity; more salt equals more shine.

morning – see opening hours, page 22). Admission charge.

NORON-LA-POTERIE

Don't be put off by the flower pots and garden gnomes stacked for sale along the busy D572 southwest of Bayeux. These hide a fine tradition of pottery-making that continues behind the shop-fronts.
9km southwest of Bayeux.

PORT RACINE

'France's smallest harbour', a tiny cove on the Cotentin Peninsula, is half the size of a football pitch with a handful of open fishing boats. Two small hotels and a house are the only signs of human habitation on this stretch of the D45 along St Martin's Bay.
On the coast, 20km northeast of Cherbourg, off the D45.

ST-LÔ

Unsympathetic rebuilding of the 'capital of the ruins' of World War II means St-

Traditional salt-glaze pottery for sale at Noron-la-Poterie, near Bayeux

The old harbour at St-Vaast-la-Hougue, a town popular for yachting and oysters

Lô is by-passed by sightseers. At the church of Notre-Dame, a bare wall fills in the bomb-damaged west front, and on the north side, a shell case remains buried in the stone. The capital of the Manche *département*, the town has a business-like air, but when the French think of St-Lô, they think of horses. The Haras, national stud, set up in 1806, has some 200 thoroughbred stallions for breeding trotters, flat race and show-jumping horses.

65km west of Caen, on the D572. Haras – rue du Maréchal Juin. Tel: 02 33 55 29 09. Open: daily May to September. Closed: weekends, May to mid-June, late September. Special displays Thursday, July, August. Telephone for details. Admission charge.

ST-VAAST-LA-HOUGUE

If the name looks foreign, thank the Scandinavian seafarers who settled around this port, which has seen plenty of action. The English landed here on their way to the battle of Crécy in 1346, and in 1692, the combined English and Dutch fleets routed the French navy. Subsequent fortifications give the port character, but today's bustle is due to the 660-berth marina (built in 1982) and a thriving oyster industry (local oysters are supposed to have a 'hint of hazelnut').

On the coast, 29km southeast of Cherbourg, off the D902.

Île de Tatihou

In 1992, to celebrate the tercentenary of the Battle of La Hougue, this island was developed into a leisure park, with nature reserve, restored military fortifications and maritime museum. Boats leave every half hour from St-Vaast.

Information – tel: 02 33 23 19 92. Admission charge.

Suspended in time ... model of parachutist
John Steele at Ste-Mère-Église

THE LONGEST DAY
(*Le jour le plus long*)
The title of Cornelius Ryan's book of
D-Day veterans' experiences was
also the title of a Hollywood film,
with international stars like John
Wayne and Robert Mitchum, Curt
Jurgens and Arletty. But the phrase
was coined by German General
Erwin Rommel. On 22 April, 1944, he
told his aide-de-camp: 'Believe me ...
the first 24 hours of the invasion will
be decisive ... the fate of Germany
will depend on it ... for the Allies,
as well as for us, this will be the
longest day.'

STE-MÈRE-ÉGLISE

Fame came to the first *commune* to be
liberated in 1944 when the film *The
Longest Day* included scenes of
paratrooper John Steele hanging by his
parachute from the 13th-century church
tower. He hung there for two hours
before being rescued by German
soldiers.

On the main square, the parachute-
shaped Musée des Troupes Aéroportées
is fascinating, with a Douglas C47 and
the Horsa glider it towed across the
English Channel, crammed with troops
of the 82nd and 101st Airborne Division.
Glass cases display the trivia of war:
occupation bank notes, undetectable
German glass mines, shaving cream, first
aid kits and moving letters home. Short
films in French and English run
continuously.
Musée des Troupes Aéroportées. Tel: 02 33

*41 41 35. Open: daily; mid-November to
mid-December weekends only (see opening
hours, page 22). Closed: mid-December to
February. Admission charge.*

Musée de la Ferme du Cotentin

Imagine the farmhands sitting round the
communal table in this 17th-century
farmhouse where cookery demon-
strations are popular with visitors. Farm
and household implements fill the 20
rooms.
*Chemin de Beauvais. Tel: 02 33 41 30 25.
Open: daily Easter to October. Admission
charge.*

*Ste-Mère-Église is 37km southeast of
Cherbourg, on the N13.*

UTAH

The code-name for the western prong
of the US attack on D-Day (see pages
86–9).

VALOGNES

The claim to be the 'Versailles of the North' requires a pinch of salt, but this attractive market town does have some grand mansions, including the 18th-century Hôtel de Beaumont opposite the cider museum. Here two huge presses are just part of the story of cider-making which goes back some five centuries. The crafts museum, in another old house, features about 20 local crafts in 15 rooms.

Musée du Calvados et des Vieux Métiers

A crafts centre-cum-museum with 18 different skills on show.
Rue Pelouze. Tel: 02 33 40 26 25. Open: daily May to October. Closed: Tuesday, May, June and September, also Sunday morning. Admission charge.

Musée du Cidre

Rue du Petit Versailles. Tel: 02 33 40 22 73. Open: daily April to October. Closed: Tuesday, Sunday morning April to June, September, October. Admission charge.

Hôtel de Beaumont

Tel: 02 33 40 12 30. Open: weekends Easter to July; daily July to September (see opening hours, page 22). Admission charge.

Valognes is 19km southeast of Cherbourg, on the N13.

VILLEDIEU-LES-POÊLES

True to its name, *poêles* (frying pans) hang in window after window along the main street, the *cuivre* (copper) glinting in the sun. Metal-working here dates back 800 years and continues today. Not only can you hear the hammering of copper but also the clanging of bells in the famous bell-foundry, as local craftsmen create everything from casseroles to carillons. There are eight attractions, all well sign-posted. A good stop for families, this is a must for food-lovers buying quality cookware.

Atelier du Cuivre (Copper Workshop)

Tel: 02 33 51 31 85. Open: Monday to Saturday. Closed: Monday in winter. Admission charge.

Fonderie de Cloches (Bell Foundry)

Tel: 02 33 61 00 56. Open: as above.

Maison de l'Étain (House of Pewter, Tin)

Tel: 02 33 51 05 08. Open: as above.

Maison du Meuble Normand (Museum of Norman Furniture)

Tel: 02 33 61 11 78. Open: daily, Easter to October; closed Tuesday morning.

Villedieu-les-Poêles is 77km southwest of Caen, on the N175.

Bell on display in the renowned foundry at Villedieu-les-Poêles

FISHING

As the cow symbolises the richness of meadows, so the fishing boat represents the harvest of the Atlantic on the doorstep. The image was captured by 19th-century painters. The reality still chugs in and out of harbours: a raised prow, a stubby mast fore and aft, a blue-smocked sailor in the 'doghouse' on the cramped deck.

Three centuries ago Norman fishermen raided the foggy Newfoundland Banks for cod. These *morutiers* (cod fishermen) salted their catch for markets throughout Europe and Dieppe, Fécamp and Honfleur grew on the profits. When France lost her Canadian territory, so the Terre-Neuve marine goldmine ran out.

Memories of this heyday of Norman fishing are never far away: museums dedicated to fishermen feature in Dieppe, Granville, Le Havre, Honfleur and, especially for Terre-Neuve, Fécamp. The annual religious ceremonies for fisherfolk have become festivals for all: Granville in February, Honfleur at

Whitsun, or Lieurey, St-Valery-en-Caux, Le Tréport and Dieppe in November during their herring festivals.

Fewer than 5,000 fishermen plough the seas now, limited by EU regulations and facing competition from Brittany, Cornwall and Ireland. Fresh fish is still sold to locals – on the beach at Etretat, by the harbour in Dieppe and on the quayside in Honfleur. *Criées* (commercial auctions) send fish off to restaurateurs all over Europe. Before

trains linked the coast to Paris, teams of horses would haul the catch, packed in seaweed, to the capital. Today, a chef as far away as the Alps can serve fish that was swimming in the sea 24 hours earlier.

Today's holidaymaker can spend a happy day casting from the beach or renting a boat to venture offshore. There are also freshwater fish in the innumerable small rivers, while chalk streams attract fly-fishermen hopefully stalking trout (see pages 160–1).

Most towns in Normandy have excellent fish markets, but if you want extra pleasure, try buying on the quayside

The Cotentin Coast

Majestic cliffs, empty beaches, 'secret' bays and small, grey-stone villages make this a delightful drive. *Allow half a day.*

From Cherbourg, take the D901 to Equeurdreville. Then follow signs and the D45 to Querqueville.

1 QUERQUEVILLE

St-Germain, the oldest chapel in western France, has survived here for 1,000 years.
Continue on the D45; at la Rivière, turn left to Château de Nacqueville.

2 URVILLE-NACQUEVILLE

The English-style gardens and 16th-century great hall of the Château de Nacqueville are open to the public (see page 141). Before Landemer stands the impressively fortified Manoir du Duc-Écu (private) with a cliff behind, the sea in front. Just past Landemer, a car-park on the right tempts visitors to admire the coastal panorama.
At the entrance to la Quiesce, a tiny right turn leads to Gruchy.

3 GRUCHY

White gates, Virginia creeper and roses on the stone cottages reflect the gentrification of this atmospheric seaside village

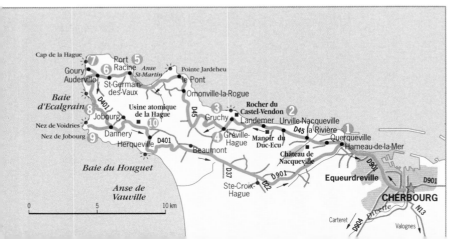

where painter Jean-François Millet was born to a peasant family in 1814.
Follow signs to Gréville-Hague on the D237.

4 GRÉVILLE-HAGUE
The stubby 12th-century village church appears in many of Millet's landscapes. His bust faces the main road.
Turn right on to the D45 to Omonville. After driving along a bramble-hedged lane, the sight of a distant power station comes as a shock. Then the road veers back towards the coast. In Omonville, turn right to le Pont, a hidden village that looks like a film set. Loop back to the D45; turn right on the coast road which has vast views of Anse St-Martin.

5 PORT RACINE
At the far end of the bay, punctuated by rocky outcrops in the water, is 'Le Plus Petit Port de France'. Port Racine is minute, just two stone jetties enclosing a dozen rowing boats tied fore and aft.
Continue on the D45. At the entrance to St-Germain turn right.

6 ST-GERMAIN-DES-VAUX
So quiet is this unspoiled village that roosters strut across the road, confident of being safe from traffic.
Turn left at the bottom of the hill on to rue Bas; left again at the T junction on to rue Joignet. Turn right on the D45. At Auderville, turn right to Goury.

7 GOURY
The road drops down to Cap de la Hague where the octagonal lifeboat station's two sets of doors enable boats to be launched into the harbour or the open sea, depending on the tides.
Return to Auderville; turn right on to the D401 (just past a hotel-restaurant).

Goury, a tiny village on the west coast of the Cotentin Peninsula

8 BAIE D'ÉCALGRAIN
The narrow road affords spectacular views over Goury and even to the Channel Islands on a clear day. Slow down after the hamlet of Écalgrain: the gorse-covered hillside plunges suddenly down to the bay and the dramatic views are distracting.
In Dannery, turn sharply right to the Nez de Jobourg.

9 NEZ DE JOBOURG
Even on a calm day, the water boils over reefs far below the cliffs of this treeless headland which is now a bird sanctuary.
Return to Dannery; rejoin the D401 for Beaumont.

10 USINE ATOMIQUE DE LA HAGUE
Behind barbed wire, the nuclear power station contrasts with the near-wilderness of the headland. Information is available in summer.
Return to Cherbourg via Beaumont.

Southern Normandy and Le Mans

*A*lthough Normandy's border may have been clearly defined for centuries, there is no dramatic change on leaving the southern *département* of Orne and entering the adjacent areas of non-Norman Mayenne and Sarthe. Mayenne, for example, has cows and half-timbered farmhouses; the local brew is cider. The cathedral and old quarter of Le Mans, capital of Sarthe, would not look out of place in a Norman city. Moreover, the whole region was fought over by the Normans and the rulers of Maine, so most towns still boast at least fragments of fortresses. Domfront, Sillé-le-Guillaume, Lassay-les-Châteaux and Mayenne have imposing ramparts; Ste-Suzanne looks impregnable on its rocky outcrop while the gatehouse of Fresnay-sur-Sarthe is a museum of peasant bonnets.

Other links include lace-making, centred on Alençon and Argentan and, above all, the love of horses. Some of the world's finest thoroughbreds, trotters, steeplechasers and showjumpers are bred here. Neat white railings signal a studfarm and grandest of all is the Haras du Pin, the French national stud, with its palatial brick offices and stables. Be there on Thursdays in summer for the musical displays. Across in the Perche region, round Nogent-le-Rotrou, the gentle *percheron* horse is king, traditionally used both in battle and farming.

This is a quiet area, with farms and the forests of Sillé and d'Écouves. Bagnoles-de-l'Orne is a spa, complete with lake and clipped lawns; more active holidaymakers take bicycles or canoes to the Alps Mancelles.

Reminders of Roman civilisation include the city wall of Le Mans, a Roman bridge across the river at Beaumont-sur-Sarthe and the ruins of baths at Jublains. Car-lovers can have their automobiles blessed at St-Christophe-le-Jajolet or watch the world-famous 24-hour race in Le Mans.

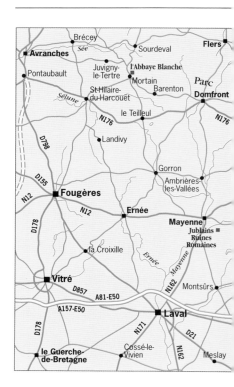

The choir of St Julien's Cathedral, from place des Jacobins, Le Mans

SOUTHERN NORMANDY

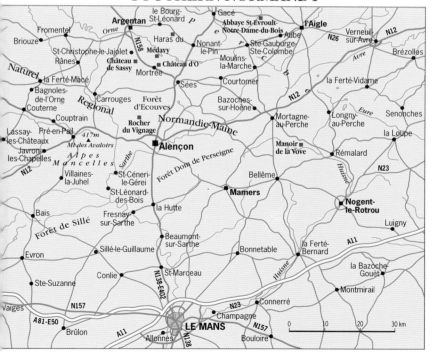

Le Mans

*T*he annual 24-hour sports car race has made Le Mans world-famous, even if few visit the old city just 3km north of the motor-racing circuit. Although Le Mans is not, and never has been, part of Normandy, its history is inextricably linked with the region. Geoffroy Le Bel, Count of Anjou and Maine and known as Geoffrey Plantagenet, was born here in 1113. He married Matilda, the grand-daughter of William the Conqueror. Their son Henri (born here in 1133) became King Henry II of England, with Normandy and Le Mans part of his realm. Queen Bérengère, widow of King Richard I of England, lived here and founded the Abbaye de l'Épau.

The hill above the River Sarthe was always an ideal position for a fort, and a reminder of early occupation is the menhir, or prehistoric stone, built into the west front of the cathedral. The Romans put a massive wall round what they called *Vindunum*. That was 1,700 years ago and some 1,300m of that enclosure were exposed in the 1980s, though why defences should be embellished with triangles, circles and diamonds of contrasting colours is still a puzzle.

From the 11th century, Le Mans wielded political, economic and religious power and so was the target of attack: by William the Conqueror in 1063; during the Hundred Years' War with England; and in the Religious Wars of the 16th century. After the French Revolution, the Royalist Vendéens took the city but were in turn crushed in a house-to-house counter-attack. Just as the city was blossoming into prosperity, the Prussians occupied it in 1870. During World War II, bombs fell after 6,000 Germans were garrisoned there.

The capital of the Sarthe *département*, Le Mans has a population of 150,000 and is known for its thriving insurance businesses and good shopping, including the indoor Centre Jacobins right by the Tourist Office.

LE MANS 24-HOUR
For information about the 24-hour race, contact Automobile Club de l'Ouest, Circuit des 24 Heures, 72019 Le Mans CEDEX. Tel: 02 43 40 24 24.

Unusual patterning on the Roman walls which surround the old city

MEN OF LE MANS
Automobiles

The Bollée family was important in the development of the automobile. Amédée senior (1844–1917) built a series of steam-driven vehicles. Amédée junior (1867–1926) designed a petrol-engined car in 1896 while Léon (1870–1913) perfected the invention and applied it to early aeroplanes. Wilbur Wright came from the USA to build and test his biplane at Le Mans. (A memorial stands on the place des Jacobins, corner of rue Wilbur Wright.)

Insurance

Le Mans' importance as an insurance centre dates back to Ariste Jacques Trouvé-Chauvel and Jean Marie Lelièvre who both started insurance companies in the 19th century.

Music

Arnold Dolmetsch (1858–1940) was responsible for the revival of interest in early music and in the instruments used to play Renaissance and baroque compositions. He popularised the recorder in schools.

LE MANS

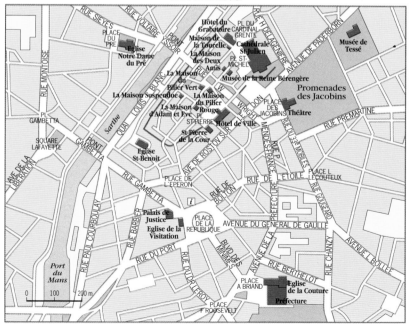

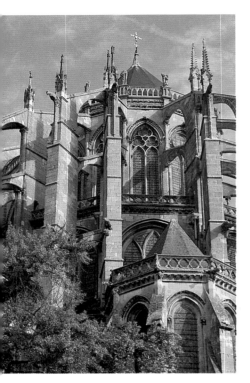

Flying buttresses leap from the 13th-century choir of the cathedral

Music flows from windows of the Conservatory of Music and Dramatic Art. Since 1986, the first weekend in July brings *Les Cénomanies*, when locals in costume (and visitors) watch strolling players with lutes, magicians doing tricks and firework displays. A walk through the ancient lanes (see pages 132–3) is delightful and proves that Le Vieux Mans is fun without being a theme park of the Middle Ages.

Cathédrale St-Julien

With no spires topping the towers and a comparatively plain west front, it is bulk, rather than height, that makes this cathedral imposing from the outside. Step inside, however, and the ceilings seem to soar: 24m high in the nave, even higher in the transept. Support comes from 54 columns, light from 169 windows.

A fire in 1134 destroyed most of the cathedral, though the side aisles survived. The new nave followed the new style – Gothic. Then in the 13th century, the canons decided the Norman choir was too narrow and dark, so the city ramparts were moved to build a 'crown of light'. The chancel and ambulatories rise to 33m, strengthened by the complex system of flying buttresses which make the east front so distinctive.

France boasts more stained glass than the rest of the world put together and St-Julien's is among the oldest. The famous Ascension Window (three along from the west door on the south side of the nave) dates from 1140, though with a few modern panes. Note the clarity of the apostles craning their necks heavenwards and the depth of colours. In 1562,

Old Le Mans

The old quarter will look familiar to Gérard Depardieu fans, since much of the film *Cyrano de Bergerac* was shot in the old cobbled streets against a backdrop of half-timbered and stone houses. Details of medieval life remain: keys carved into the pillar at La Maison du Pilier-aux-Clefs (corner Grande Rue and rue St-Honoré) told a largely illiterate population that this was the locksmith's. Much is being restored but the hustle and bustle is not just from workmen. There are cafés, restaurants and workshops for woodcarvers, jewellers, glass-blowers and artists.

during the Religious Wars, the Huguenot zealots destroyed over 50 windows; luckily many were too high to be reached. *Place St-Michel, Le Vieux Mans. Open: daily. Free.*

La Maison des Deux Amis

Between Nos 20 and 18 on the rue de la Reine Bérengère, the two friends of the title hold hands. She looks one way, he another. The large wooden shutters of No 20 would have opened up to form an awning over a shop counter.

La Maison dite de la Reine Bérengère

This house was built in 1490, 260 years after the death of Queen Bérengère, so the royal connection is less than tenuous. Carvings here and on the adjacent House of the Annunciation range from the serious (the Virgin and Archangel

Gabriel) to the fun (men squashed into tight spaces or being squeezed by a snake). Together, they house a small museum of local history, painting and ceramics.

9–13 rue de la Reine Bérengère. Tel: 02 43 47 38 51. Open: daily (see opening hours, page 22). Admission charge.

La Maison Suspendue

No prizes for translating the name of this house, with its room overhanging the street. This dates from the 16th and 17th centuries, when the advent of cannon made the medieval walls redundant, so houses were built on and below the ramparts.

Corner rue de Bouquet and rue St-Pavin de la Cité.

Carving on the tympanum over the cathedral's doorway

LES VINGT-QUATRE HEURES

Le Mans and motorsport were linked long before the 24-hour race got under way in 1923. The first ever 'Grand Prix', the *Grand Prix de l'Automobile Club de France*, was held east of the city in 1906. From the start, wealthy amateurs from all over Europe challenged for honours. After World War II, Jaguars dominated, followed by Ferrari and, in the late 1960s, the Ford GT40. Porsches battled with Matra, Jaguar made a comeback in 1988 and then Mazda of Japan challenged in 1991.

Le Mans can also mean losing and tragedy. In 1952, Pierre Levegh drove single-handed into a four-lap lead only to break down with two hours to go. In 1955, the worst accident in motor racing history occurred: 83 spectators were killed when Levegh's Mercedes hit an Austin-Healey and plunged into the crowd.

This is the beginning of the well-known Mulsanne Straight, where drivers accelerate up to 400km/h. Part of the N138, it is used by ordinary traffic travelling south the rest of the year. At Mulsanne Corner, a virtual hairpin-turn

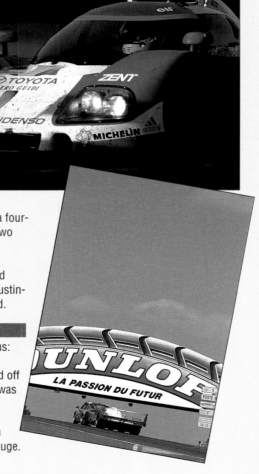

THE CIRCUIT

The Le Mans start was famous: drivers sprinted across the road, jumped into their cars and zoomed off round the 13.5km circuit but this was banned in 1969. Today, after the start, there is a right-hand bend towards the Esses before the even sharper right turn at the Tertre-Rouge.

DU MANS (LE MANS 24-HOUR RACE)

to the right, drivers watch backmarkers, brakes scream and gears crash. The fans love it. Then it's back to pits and starting line. The whole thing may last only 3½ minutes but it is repeated for 24 hours.

In and around the track, spectators barbecue and drink, brew coffee and eat croissants, go to the funfair in the centre of the track or watch the pitstops. Few stay awake throughout; nowadays, even the cars have crews of three to share the duties.

Vroom! Speed, skill and burning rubber add up to the thrills on the Le Mans circuit

CIRCUIT DES 24 HEURES DU MANS

Oldsters in the Musée de l'Automobile: left, 1909 Chenard et Walcker; right, 1910 le Zèbre Torpédo

Musée de Tessé

The city's art gallery is dedicated to the Tessé family, whose collection was confiscated after the French Revolution. As well as Greek and Egyptian antiquities, there are 14th-century religious works from Siena and paintings by Jacques-Louis David (1748–1825). The main treasure is the rare 12th-century enamel funeral portrait from the tomb of Geoffroy Le Bel.

2 avenue de Paderborn. Tel: 02 43 47 38 51. Open: daily (see opening hours, page 22). Admission charge.

Nearby:
Épau, Abbaye de l'

In the east of Le Mans, near the Lac des Sablons, this abbey was built in 1229 by Queen Bérengère and has been completely restored over the last 30 years. Today, it is best known for its annual Europa Jazz Festival (late April-early May). The queen's tomb still lies in solitary simplicity in the cloisters.

4km east of Le Mans. Tel: 02 43 84 22 29. Open: daily (see opening hours, page 22). Free.

Musée de l'Automobile

By the main entrance to the motor-racing circuit, a huge aeroplane-wing-like roof covers the hi-tech Musée de l'Automobile. Among the historic models are the 1896 Tricycle of Léon Bollée and the sleek Porsche that set a circuit record in 1971. There are videos of robots painting cars in modern factories, computer quizzes and a stomach-churning film of driving through the 'S' bends and into the Mulsanne Straight that 'makes you feel as if you're in the 24-hour race' according to one 10-year-old. Even non-aficionados find this museum interesting, thanks to clips of silly car stunts from silent movies as well as *Les Costumes des Voyageurs*: ladies' elegant silk coats, gentlemen's goggles and gloves from the early days of driving. Trivia nuts can discover which nation clocks up the most kilometres per year in private cars. Would you believe Finland?

5km south of Le Mans. Circuit des 24 Heures. Tel: 02 43 72 72 24. Open: daily (see opening hours, page 22). Closed: Tuesday from October to May. Admission charge.

LACE

To counter Venice's monopoly of making fine lace, Alençon was granted the privilege of producing lace for the French court of Louis XIV in 1665. Thanks to the invention of a new, particularly delicate and elegant *point* (stitch) with tiny bouquets of flowers, Alençon lace suddenly was in demand all over Europe. So jealously guarded was the secret of the pattern that workers only sewed separate sections, so they never knew the complete 'code'. A school of lace maintains the tradition.

ALENÇON

The capital of the Orne *département* used to be synonymous with fine lace; today, Moulinex hairdryers and food processors give the town its prosperity. The rue du Bercail and Grande-Rue are pleasant old streets that intersect outside the 14th-century church of Notre-Dame. Other landmarks include a chapel dedicated to Ste Thérèse, born here in 1873. The medieval Ozé House is now the tourist office.

Musée de la Dentelle

A short film in English is available to explain the town's tradition of lace-making. Then compare the handmade lace from Alençon with examples from the rest of the world.
31 rue du Pont-Neuf. Tel: 02 33 26 27 26. Open: Monday to Saturday (see opening hours, page 22). Admission charge.

Fine lace on show in Alençon's
Musée de la Dentelle

Alençon is 48km north of Le Mans, on the N138.

ARGENTAN

A rival to Alençon (45km away), Argentan had its own particular lace pattern which was rediscovered by chance in the local archives in 1864. Now the copyright belongs to Benedictine nuns at the local abbey. La Maison des Dentelles in the rue de la Noë explains all (open daily). Somehow, the town's two old churches, St-Germain and St-Nicolas, survived the devastation of the summer of 1944, but most of Argentan has been rebuilt.
58km southeast of Caen, on the N158.

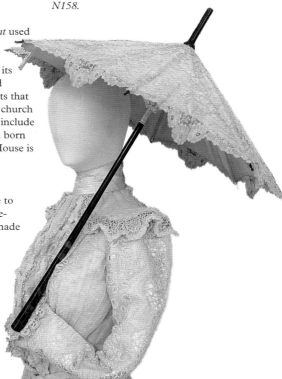

The château at Bagnoles-de-l'Orne adds
to the attractions of this famous spa town

with the surrounding forest, make this
a peaceful place for holidaymakers,
whether or not they take the cure.
38km southwest of Argentan, off the D916.

BEAUMONT-SUR-SARTHE

The tranquil setting belies this town's
tempestuous past. William the
Conqueror won and lost it three times,
and it was fought over by subsequent
lords and monarchs. Lumps of the castle
walls, demolished in 1617, remain.
Don't miss the low-slung Roman bridge
near the weir.
23km south of Alençon, on the N138.

Prieuré de Vivoin

Two kilometres to the east, the
handsome 13th-century priory and
church with its Hall of Pillars is a tribute ·
to volunteers who restored the ravages of
time and the French Revolution. In
summer, there are evening concerts.
*Tel: 02 43 97 04 36. Open: afternoons daily,
March to November. Admission charge.*

CARROUGES, CHÂTEAU DE

King Louis XI slept here ... back in
August 1473. His hosts, the Le Veneur
family, had already been here for a
century. They left in 1936 but this
red-brick, rectangular castle is still
impressive, protected by deep moats and
with a fairy-tale gatehouse with steep
slate roofs. In the grounds are a craft
centre as well as the visitors' centre for
the Normandy-Maine Regional Nature
Park, spread out below the château and
the village.
*29km northwest of Alençon, on the D909.
Tel: 02 33 27 20 32. Open: daily (see
opening hours, page 22). Admission charge.*

BAGNOLES-DE-L'ORNE

Great claims are made for the springs at
this spa town: one legend tells how an
old horse called Rapide was the first to
benefit, while according to another, a
monk delighted by his treatment jumped
the 4m-gap between two rocks high
above the water. The spot is still known
as the *Saut du Capucin* (Monk's Leap).
The *Grande Source* (Big Spring) jets out
water at 25°C for body-pummelling
showers as well as for drinking. Sufferers
from rheumatic and vascular complaints
are said to gain most. Neat and tidy, with
a lake, racecourse, casino and park, it has
obvious attractions for the older
generation, but the campsite, 9-hole golf
course and good rock climbing, together

DOMFRONT

On a clear day, the view from the fortress over the Passais region stretches to Mont Marganfin, some 13km to the south. When England's King Henry II and his love, Eleanor of Aquitaine, held court here in the 12th century, this was a fearsome stronghold. Now only a few thick walls in the public gardens remain, though from rue des Fossés-Plisson you can still see where towers jutted up from the medieval ramparts. The narrow rue du Docteur-Barrabé still has half-timbered houses and Notre-Dame-sur-l'Eau has had some of its 12th-century beauty restored, including the frescos. Damage here was not from the war but from 19th-century road builders.

36km north of Mayenne, on the D962.

ÉVRON

Every year, on the first weekend in September, the _Festival de la Viande_ (Festival of Meat) features some of the finest flesh in France to the delight of the chefs' _Confrérie de l'Entrecôte_ (Brotherhood of Steak). The rest of the year, the Gothic basilica is the draw for pilgrims who pray at the 13th-century, silver-covered, carved wooden figure of Notre-Dame de l'Épine (Our Lady of the Thorn).

57km northwest of Le Mans, off the A81.

One of the fine state rooms at Château de Carrouges

FERTÉ-MACÉ, LA

If Évron is all about beef, this town is all about tripe, prepared *en brochette*, using *gras-double*, three of the four stomachs of the cow, wrapped round pieces of cow foot and cooked on a kebab-like wooden skewer. Eat them as locals do at the Thursday morning open-air market.
46km northwest of Alençon, on the D916.

FRESNAY-SUR-SARTHE

The main town of the Alpes Mancelles, Fresnay has a medieval quarter with cobbled streets, ancient houses and the remains of defences against Normandy. The postern-gate with its twin towers now houses the Musée des Coiffes, devoted to headwear. Through the gate, a garden leads to sheer walls above the River Sarthe. The town makes a good base for exploring the quiet Sarthe Valley and the forest of Sillé.

Headdress from the Auvergne (in the south) in Fresnay's Musée des Coiffes

Musée des Coiffes

Tel: 02 43 97 22 20. Open: weekends, holidays March to September; daily July, August. Admission charge.

Fresnay-sur-Sarthe is 20km southwest of Alençon, off the N138.

JUBLAINS RUINES ROMAINES

These Roman ruins are in the middle of nowhere; fields stretch in all directions,

and Mayenne is some 10km away. Excavations are slowly revealing more clues to this square Roman fort. An audio-visual display explains how the hot and cold baths (which can be clearly seen) used to work.
14km northwest of Évron, on the D7. Tel: 02 43 04 30 16. Open: Tuesday to Sunday (see opening hours, page 22). Closed: February. Admission charge.

LASSAY-LES-CHÂTEAUX

Marked 'Lassay' on most maps, the full name refers to the three castles in the immediate area. Without being unkind to the châteaux of Bois-Thibault and Bois-Frou, it is the fortress in Lassay itself that attracts military historians as well as children. For over 500 years, its draw-bridge, barbican, ramparts and eight stubby, circular towers have dominated the surrounding countryside.
16km southwest of Bagnoles-de-l'Orne, on the D34. Tel: 02 43 04 74 33. Open: weekends Easter to May; daily June to September. Admission charge.

LAVAL

Outside the old walls, the *préfecture* (capital) of the Mayenne *département* is a modern city; within are twisting streets with half-timbered houses clustering around what is left of the old castle. Here, the museum honours favourite son Henri Rousseau, the 19th-century painter nicknamed '*Le Douanier*', with a large international collection of Naïve Art. Although displaying only one of his paintings, it does have his reconstructed studio, complete with paint box and easel. Rousseau was born in the south tower of the Porte Beucheresse, the old city gate which still stands. His grave in La Perrine Park bears a moving inscription, carved as if handwritten, by the poet

A near-perfect fortress – the Château de Lassay, most impressive of the three castles

Apollinaire, an admirer of his work.

From the 16th to 18th centuries, Laval was an important textile-producing town, and mansions like the Maison du Grand Veneur (Master of the Royal Hunt's House) at the corner of the Grand Rue and rue des Orfèvres attest to its prosperity. Another is the Maison de Clermont at No 8 rue de la Trinité, where six statuettes parade across the façade.

Bateau-Lavoir 'Le Saint-Julien'
This turn-of-the-century floating laundry, with big copper kettles, was in use until 1970!
Tel: 02 43 49 46 46. Open: July, August, Tuesday to Sunday. Admission charge.

Musée du Vieux Château
Tel: 02 43 53 39 89. Open: Tuesday to Sunday (see opening hours, page 22). Admission charge.

Laval is 83km west of Le Mans, off the A81.

MAYENNE
Although in the *département* of Mayenne and astride the River Mayenne, this small, quiet town is best known as the starting and finishing point for boating holidays. The crumbling fortress on the west bank is undergoing a massive face-lift which will last several years. Mansions on the place Cheverus and place de Hercé may be admired from the outside only since they are private. This is a place for strolling rather than for staying.
88km northwest of Le Mans, via the A81, N162.

Covered excavations at the Roman fort of Jublains

MORTAGNE-AU-PERCHE

Weekends bring Parisians to this hilly and misty region, that gave its name to the sturdy Percheron horses bred from Saracen stallions abandoned by the Moors in the 8th century. Mortagne itself is famous for *boudin* (see box) and kilometres of it are sold during the annual Black Pudding Fair mid-way through Lent. In the flamboyant Gothic church of Notre-Dame, a stained-glass window commemorates locals who settled in Canada in the 17th century.

Maison des Comtes du Perche/ Musée Alain

'I am a Percheron, that's to say, different from a Norman,' said Emile Chartier. The museum pays tribute to this philosopher, known simply as 'Alain', who was born here in 1868.
8 rue du Portail-St-Denis. Tel: 02 33 25 25 87. Open: afternoons Tuesday to Saturday. Free.

Musée Percheron

Tel: 02 33 25 25 87. Open: afternoons July, August. Closed: Monday. Free.

Mortagne-au-Perche is 38km east of Alençon, off the N12.

NOGENT-LE-ROTROU

During the French Revolution, many symbols of the aristocracy were destroyed, so it is a tribute to the Duc de Sully (who died in 1641) that his tomb in the Hôtel-Dieu remained unharmed. King Henri IV's chief minister was admired for his support for French farmers, declaring that the 'real gold mines of France were her *bourage* (ploughing) and *pastourage* (meadows)'. In the ruined castle, the Musée du Perche records local life.

> ### BOUDIN
>
> Mortagne's gift to French rural cuisine, *boudin* (black pudding), is a gourmet speciality made from pig's blood and coiled like a black rubber hose. With forests full of wild pigs, the Percheron peasants had ample opportunity to develop their skills in *charcuterie*. To preserve this heritage, the Confrèrie des Chevaliers du Goûte-Boudin (the Knights of the Black Pudding Brotherhood) invented a Black Pudding Fair in 1963. Surprise! – entries from England and Scotland scooped some of the top prizes.

Not a headless snake, but *boudin*, the speciality of Mortagne

Nogent-le-Rotrou is 74km northeast of Le Mans, on the N23.

O, CHÂTEAU D'

As romantic as any château of the Loire Valley, this has a fairy-tale quality, with its steep roofs and enclosing moat. Its three wings embody three periods of architecture: the 15th century (east wing), 16th century (south wing) and 18th century (west wing). Despite the brevity of the surname, the O family was, for four generations, one of the most powerful in France, from Jean d'O, a counsellor to King Charles VII at the end of the 15th century to François d'O, finance minister a century later to both King Henri III and King Henri IV. Renovations inside have recently revealed *trompe-l'oeil* paintings. The Salon des Muses is painted with life-like statues of goddesses, while in the adjacent gallery visitors crane their necks to admire swooping eagles.

Near Mortrée, 15km southeast of Argentan. Tel: 02 33 35 35 27. Open: Wednesday to Monday afternoons.

PIN, HARAS DU

Jules Hardouin-Mansart, 17th-century architect, who remodelled Versailles, also designed this 'Versailles of the Horse'. Away from main roads, on the edge of an oak forest, France's most famous national stud is a pink-brick mansion and stables enclosing a courtyard of lawn and gravel paths. Today's residents include some of the world's finest stallions: thoroughbred for racing and trotting, saddle-horses for showjumping and Anglo-Arabs for steeplechasing. Even the ancient Percheron breed has been preserved. But the Haras does more than produce

Fittingly splendid gateway to the national stud of Haras du Pin

champions; it also trains people, from grooms to breeders, to continue the traditions of France's 22 studs.

A brisk guided tour is available all year round but even better are the *musicales du jeudi*, the Thursday afternoon practice sessions, conducted to music in summer. Guided tours every half-hour.

12km east of Argentan, on the N26. Tel: 02 33 36 68 68. Open: daily. Admission charge.

The River Sarthe making its way through St-Cénéri-le-Gérei

ST-CÉNÉRI-LE-GÉREI

No wonder this hamlet is crowded with visitors in the height of summer: its title of 'one of the most beautiful villages in France' is fully justified. Cottages sit on a small rocky outcrop above the burbling River Sarthe, while the small church with its saddleback roof at the top of the village has bold 13th-century frescos in the choir. The artist Corot came here over a century ago and today there are still artists' studios where the painters

and potters who live here year round show off their wares.

53km northwest of Le Mans, on the D101.

ST-CHRISTOPHE-LE-JAJOLET

If you want to have your car blessed, be here the last Sunday in July or the first Sunday in October and join the procession of cars past the church dedicated to St Christopher, patron saint of travellers. Inside the church, note the delightful mural of a 1920s goggled driver and pilot.

8km south of Argentan, off the N158.

Château de Sassy

The building of this mansion was interrupted by the Revolution: no doubt the owner, the lawyer of King Louis XVI, was attending his client in prison. The monarch lost his head but a lock of his hair is here, along with a legal library amassed by the Pasquier family over the centuries. The classic formal gardens are famous (see page 141).

Detail from the mural in the church of St-Christophe-le-Jajolet

The quiet interior of Maison Fouquet,
at Ste-Suzanne

*Tel: 02 33 35 32 66. Gardens – open: daily.
Free. Château – open: afternoons daily from
Palm Sunday to October. Admission charge.*

ST-LÉONARD-DES-BOIS
In the heart of the Alpes Mancelles, the
River Sarthe loops past the Grand
Fourché, a towering, wooded
escarpment, then rounds a meadow
which in summer is a busy campsite.
This hamlet of stone houses makes a
good base for hiking well-marked trails.
Despite its name, the Vallée de Misère
(the Vale of Tears) provides an enjoyable
morning walk past the Manoir de Linthe
and through unspoilt countryside.
49km northwest of Le Mans, on the D258.

STE-SUZANNE
Not many fortresses got the better of
William the Conqueror, but after a four-
year siege here, he finally gave up. The
triangular outcrop of rock 70m above the
River Erve was taken by the English
during the Hundred Years' War, but the
French won it back 15 years later, thanks
to the help of an Englishman married to
a local girl. Ste Suzanne is, incidentally,
the patron saint of fiancés/fiancées.
Today, shops and art galleries huddle
below the castle's huge walls which
protect a church and restored buildings,
including the Musée de l'Auditoire
(Audience Chamber Museum), whose
display of weights and measures through
the ages ranges from shoe sizers to
opium scales. Built into the ramparts is
the elegant yet plain 17th-century
country house of Fouquet de la Varenne,
inventor of the French postal service.
*50km west of Le Mans, off the A81, on the
D7. Musée de l'Auditoire. Tel: 02 43 01 42*

*16. Open: May to October, afternoons
daily. Admission charge.*

SÉES
British tourists often stop here after a
ferry crossing to Caen, perhaps attracted
by the red telephone box across from the
13th-century cathedral. Beneath the two
spires resembling inverted ice-cream
cones is a clear, uncluttered nave with no
side chapels. A tape-recorded history,
backed with organ music, leaps into life
at the touch of a button: the acoustics are
superb.
22km north of Alençon, on the N138.

SILLÉ-LE-GUILLAUME
Spilling down a very steep hillside, Sillé
is dominated by a massive 15th-century
castle that looks even more menacing
than William the Conqueror's original
fortress. Built to protect Maine from the
Normans, the keep stands 40m high,
complete with machicolations. Nowadays, however, the nearby lake and forest
of Sillé draw visitors for sailing, cycling
and walking.
32km northwest of Le Mans, on the D304.

The Alpes Mancelles

The 'alps of Le Mans' recently celebrated their centenary as a recognised tourist attraction. These tumbling hills, with forests and attractive villages, are on the southern fringe of Normandy. Although this quiet, scenic route is only 24km, it is a stern test for gears and thighs. *Allow 3 hours.*

Take the N12 west from Alençon; follow signs to the Alpes Mancelles and begin the route at St-Pierre-des-Nids.

1 ST-PIERRE-DES-NIDS

Many cyclists stay in M Etienne's *auberge*, Le Dauphin, directly opposite the church. Thanks to a local campaign, the bells are

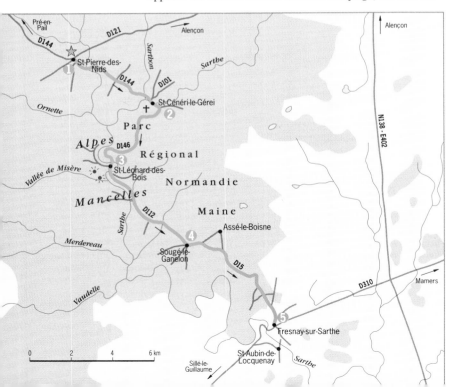

silent at night ... to the benefit of tourists and locals alike.

Leave the village on the D144 towards St-Cénéri-le-Gérei.

2 ST-CÉNÉRI-LE-GÉREI

After a roller-coaster ride through fields and farms, the road leads up to St-Cénéri. Perched on a hill, this artists' colony of carefully-restored stone cottages revels in the designation 'one of the prettiest villages in France'. Not only the art galleries but also some of the studios are open to the public; watch an artist or craftsman at work, then pause at a café before climbing up to the simple 12th-century church with its old frescos, tombs built into the walls and vistas over the valleys.

Take the D146 to St-Léonard-des-Bois. After a short, steep descent out of St-Cénéri, the road crosses the River Sarthe; glance right for a view of the church, with the cliff dropping away below. Then continue through open fields and thick chestnut woods, past high hedges and farms selling goat cheese.

3 ST-LÉONARD-DES-BOIS

Four steep hills overlook the River Sarthe as it curves past this village. Thick woods give way to open water-meadows and the bridge is adorned with flower boxes and collectors of churches can add another 12th-century one to their list. The small population swells in summer thanks to the campsite, and there are several places for refreshment or for purchasing the makings of a picnic.

Continue on the D112 to Sougé-le-Ganelon. As the road flattens, look right for the Manoir de Linthe. Dating from the 11th century, the round tower was originally a dovecot. Follow the River Sarthe, watching for fishermen in waders casting for trout.

4 SOUGÉ-LE-GANELON

The horizon is broken by the spire of the hilltop church. Apricot-coloured houses on the edge of the village contrast with the covered public wash-house, complete with pump, half-way up to the main square.

Follow signs in the village to the D15 and Fresnay. The road follows the ridge of hills, with the river glittering below.

5 FRESNAY-SUR-SARTHE

Locals claim their church resembles Mont-St-Michel ... from a distance. Behind it is the ancient heart of town, with narrow, cobbled streets and small shops. The old market hall in the place Thiers has been preserved and cleverly glassed in. A sculpture-cum-fountain of a lion and a tree represents the town's coat of arms. The open place de la Mairie leads to twin towers housing a museum of headwear (see page 124). Beyond is a public garden and the ruins of battlements above the sheer drop to the river.

The route ends here. There are cafés and hotels for refreshment or to stay the night.

Old Le Mans

With its half-timbered buildings and narrow lanes, the medieval quarter of Le Mans deserves a whole roll of film. Remember to look up to spot decorative carvings and down for sure footing on the cobbles. *Allow 45 minutes.*

Start in the place St-Michel. Pass the cathedral entrance and continue to the northwest corner of the building where a menhir stands at the base. This pagan relic symbolises the old religion, displaced by Christianity.

1 RUE DES CHANOINES

Immediately on the right is No 27, the Maison de la Tourelle, rich with carvings including a beast's face at the bottom of the water pipe. It is now the bishop's house, but the cellar was once home to a 'lady of ill repute'.

Continue along the street. Opposite the wrought-iron gate of No 26 is a tiny statue in a niche: St Sebastian with an arrow piercing his side. Further along, La Maison Saint-Martin houses a jeweller, one of many craftsmen in this area.

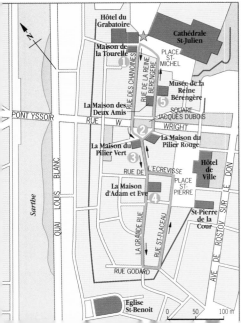

2 SQUARE JACQUES DUBOIS

Imagine standing here centuries ago, ready to defend the city. Far below flows the River Sarthe and across lies modern Le Mans. In the 19th century, a tunnel was dug through the hillside to improve access to the city.

Cross the square with its gardenia trees to two houses facing each other at the start of La Grande Rue.

3 LA GRANDE RUE

On the right is La Maison du Pilier Vert; opposite, La Maison du Pilier Rouge with flecks of red paint still on the pillar. The carved skull and sticks were once thought to denote the house of the executioner, but he lived elsewhere and the sticks were for an annual sporting contest won by the first to hit a ball over the cathedral.

The massive red wooden pillar gives this building its name, La Maison du Pilier Rouge

Continue down the street, past the Conservatory of Music and Dramatic Art. Look at the pillar on the corner of rue de l'Écrevisse. The three huge stones prevented carriage wheels damaging the house.

4 LA MAISON D'ADAM ET ÈVE

Decide for yourself whether it is Adam and Eve above the doorway or perhaps Bacchus. Look up to see the woman riding a centaur while four musicians provide music. Fish and a man-in-the-moon represent the interests of the original owner, a royal astrologer.
Continue downhill, noting the keys on the pillar of La Maison du Pilier-aux-Clefs. Look into courtyards, peep through gates. Turn left into the tiny rue Godard and left again into the rue St-Flaceau, built atop the city ramparts. Walk past the cafés in the place St-Pierre, go left on the rue de

l'Ecrevisse. At la Grande Rue, return uphill, crossing the square on to the rue de la Reine Bérengère.

5 RUE DE LA REINE BÉRENGÈRE

Statues of a man and woman hold hands above the doorways to Nos 18 and 20, where wooden shutters once opened to display the shop's wares. Step through the entrance to the Musée de la Reine Bérengère and into a second courtyard for a dramatic view of the cathedral, then continue along the street, admiring more carvings. At the Maison de l'Annonciation, the Virgin awaits the Archangel Gabriel, perhaps amused by the two men with sore necks and five men entwined by a serpent.
Continue along the street back to the cathedral.

KING HAROLD'S REVENGE

The English have long been regular visitors to Normandy. Many drive through to points further south, others settle in for holidays. In the past 10 years, however, a new breed has emerged: the property owner. With the abolition of currency exchange controls and the freedom of movement permitted within the European Union, cross-border

house purchases became straightforward. So, when property prices in southern England sky-rocketed in the 1980s, English families searching for second homes looked to Normandy, where prices seemed a bargain.

The younger generation of Normans were leaving the land to live in towns; the older generation wanted comfortable modern villas; neither wanted to keep up the old family home in the country. The English, however, are passionate about 'doing up' houses ... the older the better. Although there has been some resentment, relations are generally good; often a neighbouring farmer keeps an eye on the house in exchange for using a field or collecting apples from the orchard. The English come for holidays and lend their *résidences secondaires* (second homes) to friends; some have become permanent residents, joining in the life of the local community.

Purchasing a house is simple. Some French *agences immobilières* (estate agents) specialise in overseas sales. The local *notaire* (notary) oversees the *sous-seing privé* (private agreement) between buyer and seller that is both more binding and expedited more quickly than the English equivalent.

The English on their overcrowded island are also lured by recreation facilities. New golf courses have been carved out of the lush pastureland; queues are unknown. While 'full' signs may be common in England's south coast marinas, Normandy has built some 20 *ports de plaisance* with 10,000 berths to attract British sailors. With the recession, the impetus has lessened but the tide has not turned.

Signs of the times – the foreign invasion of France

GETTING AWAY FROM IT ALL

'The view is superb, the sea always the sea! ... This sea is something totally different from the Mediterranean, at one and the same time mean and great.'

ÉMILE ZOLA
Zest for Life, 1875

Getting Away From it All

BEACHES

Normandy's beaches have attracted sea-bathers for nearly two centuries. Sadly, the heavy traffic in the English Channel has led to heavy pollution all along the coasts on both sides of the water. The French Government carries out tests in accordance with European Union regulations and grades the quality of the beaches. Category A beaches have 'good-quality water conforming with EU directives'. All but one of these are in the Manche *département*. Beaches are listed by nearest town/village and location.

MANCHE

From the southeast, going anticlockwise round the peninsula, these are the best beaches. Many are opposite or at the end of small roads that lead to the sea.

Ste-Marie-du-Mont
Utah Beach
St-Martin-de-Varreville
by the Monument Leclerc
St-Germain-de-Varreville
opposite D129 road
St-Marcouf-de-l'Isle
Les Gougins beach
St-Vaast-la-Hougue
La Hougue beach
Barfleur
La Sambière beach

Gouberville
Le Bas de la Rue
Néville
opposite D514 road
Réthoville
opposite D226 road
Cosqueville
Le Vicq beach
Fermanville
Anse de la Mondrée bay,
Anse du Brick bay
Bretteville en Sarthe
beach

Querqueville
by the Camping des
Armées campsite
Les Pieux
Sciotot beach
Le Rozel
opposite campsite
Surtainville
opposite D66 road
Beaubigny
opposite D131 road
Barneville-Carteret
north side of the
promontory
St-Jean-de-la-Rivière
opposite D166
Portbail
opposite CRS post
St-Lô-d'Ourville
Lindbergh-Plage beach
St-Rémy-des-Landes
opposite D327 road
Surville
opposite D526 road
Glatigny
opposite D337 road
Bretteville-sur-Ay
opposite D136 road
Pirou
opposite D94 road
Agon-Coutainville
central beach

LAKES AND INLAND WATERS
The same controls govern inland water facilities, with the same categories, from A to D (pass to fail).

The cleanest are:	Orne	Base Plein Air et Loisirs-
Calvados	La Ferté	Zone Verte
Pont-l'Évêque	Brochardière	**Manche**
Plan d'eau de Pont-	**Eure**	Le Val-St-Père
l'Évêque	Poses	at le Gué-de-l'Épine

Annoville
opposite D537 road
Lingreville
opposite D220 road
Bréhal
opposite D592 road
Coudeville
opposite D351 road
Granville
Le Plat Gousset beach
Jullouville
Les Sapins beach, Carolles beach
Champeaux
Sol Roc beach

SEINE-MARITIME
Veulettes-sur-Mer
Veulettes beach

European Blue Flag awards
Ten Normandy beaches boast the
highest honours:
Dieppe (Dieppe Plage)
Veules-les-Roses
Merville Francville Plage
Ouistreham
Courseulles-sur-Mer
Néville-sur-Mer
Barneville-Carteret
St-Georges-de-la-Rivière
Bréhal
Bréville-sur-Mer.

NATIONAL PARKS
Normandy has three national parks.

PARC NATUREL RÉGIONAL DE BROTONNE
The park's heart is the Forêt de
Brotonne itself, a vast beech forest
south of Caudebec-en-Caux. The
protected area, however, is much larger,
a total of 58,000 hectares. On the south
bank of the Seine, pretty drives include
the Route des Chaumières (the Cottage
Trail), signposted between La
Mailleraye-sur-Seine and the Vernier
Marshes. A dozen small 'eco-museums'
feature the traditions of the Brotonne.

Maison du Parc (Park Service HQ)
Notre-Dame-de-Bliquetuit, southeast of the
Pont-de-Brotonne. Tel: 02 35 37 23 16.
Open: daily April to October; weekdays
November to March.

Maison de la Pomme (Apple Museum)
This museum examines the role of the
apple in Norman life.
Ste-Opportune-la-Mare. Tel: 02 32 57 16
48. Open: daily. Admission charge.

The Forge
Ste-Opportune-la-Mare. Tel: 02 32 57 16
48. Open: Sunday afternoons May to
August. Admission charge.

Maison du Lin (Flax Museum)

Everything you ever wanted to know about flax for making linen. Upper Normandy is one of Europe's leading producers.

Routot. Tel: 02 32 56 21 76. Open: weekends April to October. Admission charge.

Maison des Métiers (Crafts Museum and Workshops)

Patchwork in the museum and nearby studios is just one craft on show at this well-presented centre of traditional farming techniques. On Sundays craftsmen demonstrate their skills.

Bourneville. Tel: 02 35 57 40 41. Open: afternoons April to October; all day July, August. Admission charge for museum.

Four à Pain (Bread Oven)

Claude Dambry makes crusty loaves the old-fashioned way every Sunday from March to November in this museum of country baking.

La Haye-de-Routot. Tel: 02 32 57 07 99. Open: Sunday afternoons March to October; weekend afternoons April to June; daily afternoons July, August. Admission charge.

Musée du Sabotier (Clogmakers' Museum)

France's only collection of *sabots* (clogs) both from this region and neighbouring countries. A film shows how clogs were made.

La Haye-de-Routot. Tel: 02 32 57 59 67. Open: as Four à Pain; one admission ticket covers both attractions.

Beech glades in Perseigne Forest, east of Alençon, a haven of peace and quiet

L'Apiculteur (the Beekeeper)

M and Mme Lurel demonstrate the world of the bee through the special window of their beehive.

Mesnil-sous-Jumièges. Le Halage – tel: 02 35 91 36 76. Open: afternoons April to October. Admission charge.

Moulin de Pierre (Windmill)

Given enough wind, this restored stone windmill grinds flour as it did in the 13th century. The former Miller's House reflects the importance of this traditional form of energy.

Hauville. Tel: 02 35 37 23 16. Open: Sunday afternoons March, April, October to mid-November; weekend afternoons May, June and September; afternoons July and August.

MARAIS DU COTENTIN ET DU BESSIN

Local villages have combined to preserve 120,000 hectares of this important breeding ground for flora and fauna. The marshes, rich grazing ground in spring and summer, usually flood in autumn and winter, so dikes and elevated roads are a feature. The 25,000 hectares of marshes surrounding Carentan are on the eastern side of the Cotentin 'neck', where rivers like the Douve and Taute flow to the sea. On the migration route between Northern Europe and Africa, these marshes are a paradise for birdwatchers. There are boat trips along the canals and rivers, even horse-drawn caravan rides in summer.

St-Lô. Tel: 02 33 05 68 04.

PARC NATUREL RÉGIONAL DE NORMANDIE-MAINE

Like Brotonne, this 234,000-hectare area embraces heritage as well as nature. There are 45,000 hectares of mainly

Fan-tailed warbler

beech forest like Andaine, Écouves, Mortain, Perseigne and Sillé, as well as classic small, hedged fields of the *bocage*. Add in the rocky outcrops and gorges, lakes and rivers, and this is a peaceful, if popular, place for lovers of the outdoors.

Maison du Parc

Full details of all the activities available can be had from the park headquarters in Carrouges.

BP05, 61320 Carrouges. Tel: 02 33 81 75 75.

Canoeing: on the Sarthe, Mayenne and Varenne Rivers.

Cycling, riding and walking: on marked trails through the park.

Rock climbing: in Andaine forest there are rock faces specially designated for climbers; in Mortain, the Aiguille (needle) and the Fosse-Arthour gully are well-known challenges for climbers.

Statue of the artist Monet among the flowers at Giverny

GARDENS

The Normans are keen gardeners. Cottages have tidy plots of vegetables and flowers; châteaux, of course, have specially designed terraces, beds and parks. Some of these show the influence of English neighbours across the Channel, others look to Italy and Holland; most, however, are in the great French tradition of horticulturalists like André Le Nôtre.

Beaumesnil

Château de Beaumesnil boasts a 350-year-old garden designed by Le Nôtre's contemporary, Jean de la Quintinie. As well as the classic formal garden there is a box tree maze on a ruined keep and a mirror lake (see page 65).

Tel: 02 32 44 40 09. Open: daily Easter to 1 November. Closed: Tuesday. Admission charge.

Beaumont-Hague

The Château de Vauville garden could be on the Côte d'Azur rather than the English Channel, thanks to its collection of bamboo and yucca, agave and aloe. *Tel: 02 33 52 71 41. Open: afternoons Sunday and Tuesday, May to October. Admission charge.*

Caen

The 250-year-old Jardin des Plantes is the city's pride and joy, along with the Vallée des Jardins near by. It's worth checking out the guided tours that take place on some Saturday afternoons.

5 *place Biot. Tel: 02 31 30 42 63. Open: daily. Free.*

Giverny
Claude Monet Gardens (see page 42).

Martinvast
The Parc de Beaurepaire has 175-year-old gardens laid out in the English style, with streams, waterfalls and lakes. Thanks to the nearby Gulf Stream, exotica like tulip trees and palm trees thrive.
Tel: 02 33 52 02 23. Open: afternoons April to November. Admission charge.

Mézidon
The De Mézerac family have toiled long and hard to make the Château de Canon garden into one of Normandy's gems. It has a scarlet Chinese pavilion and a ruined castle, a reflecting pool and the Chartreuses walled gardens.
Tel: 02 31 20 02 72. Open: weekends and holidays Easter to June; afternoons July to September. Closed: Tuesday. Admission charge.

Offranville
Visitors who pay homage to the writer Guy de Maupassant at the Château de Miromesnil can also enjoy an authentic Victorian-style kitchen garden with vegetables and flowers carefully interspersed (see pages 44–5).
Tel: 02 35 85 02 80. Open: May to mid-October, Wednesday to Monday daily. Admission charge.

St-Christophe-le-Jajolet
The Château de Sassy typifies the formal French garden, where nature

conforms to order. Box hedges are clipped, even trees are controlled.
Tel: 02 33 35 32 66. Open: afternoons Easter to November. Free.

Urville-Nacqueville
West of Cherbourg, the Château de Nacqueville boasts an English garden in a sheltered valley. Azaleas and rhododendrons surround the lake; lilies border a tinkling stream.
Tel: 02 33 03 27 89. Open: Easter to October, Wednesday, Thursday and Saturday to Monday. Admission charge.

Varengeville-sur-Mer
The Parc Floral des Moutiers on the Dieppe cliffs was designed by the influential landscape gardener Gertrude Jekyll. The magnolias are outstanding.
8km west of Dieppe. Tel: 02 35 85 10 02. Open: daily mid-March to mid-November. Admission charge.

Le Vastérival is the creation of the Danish Princess Sturdza in 1957. There are already over 1,000 species of flowers, juxtaposed carefully for the greatest effect.
1km west of Varengeville on D75. Tel: 02 35 85 12 05. Open: daily (by appointment only). Admission charge.

The bridge and water lilies at Giverny – Monet's inspiration

A typical Normandy beech forest; this is Perseigne, Vallée d'Enfer

Fallencourt and Foucarmont. The middle of the *département*, inland from Dieppe, boasts the forest of Eawy (pronounced Ee-ah-vy). Use the small town of St-Saëns as a base to explore the 6,500 hectares of timberland. Straddling the border with Eure is Normandy's largest and, arguably, France's best beech forest: the Forêt de Lyons (11,000 hectares), with the charming Lyons-la-Forêt at its heart. Some 9km north, on the N31, is the famous Hêtre de la Bunodière, an ancient tree some 40m tall.

Eure

A mixture of beech, pine and oak, the Brotonne Forest is in the Parc Naturel Regional de Brotonne (Brotonne National Park – see pages 137–9). Although near Rouen and accessed now by the massive Pont de Brotonne, it can swallow up even national-holiday crowds, particularly away from the eco-museums.

Orne

The forest of Andaine, part of the Normandy-Maine Regional Nature Park, is between Bagnoles-de-l'Orne and Juvigny. The fit can admire the 5,300 hectares from the top of the observation tower of Bonvouloir on the D235. Another tower is in the middle of the forest of Écouves, north of Alençon: 8,000 hectares of mixed woodland, full of deer.

Sarthe

East of Alençon is the Perseigne Forest, full of beech glades that will call up that 'cathedral-like' description once again.

FORESTS

'Cathedral-like' is an over-used cliché to describe forests but in Normandy it is actually true. Standing tall and straight, the *hêtres* (beech) could be the columns of a nave, their spreading leaves the roof. Some woods are small, for example by the abbey around Cérisy-la-Forêt, but there are half-a-dozen over 5,000 hectares, all with roads for cars and paths for walking.

Seine-Maritime

In northeastern Normandy there are over 9,000 hectares of beech trees: the *haute* (upper) and *basse* (lower) forests of Eu, separated by the villages of

DIRECTORY

'Now we are on Dieppe
beach: on the pebbles. A
bottle of Muscadet, a
portion of frites, pâté de
campagne, bread, goat
cheese and cherries.'
DAVID HOLBROOK
A Day in France

Shopping

*A*s in the rest of France, food is top of the shopping list. Despite the rise of the hypermarket, specialist shops are still an important part of French life.

Types of shops

Boucherie: the butcher's shop, where everything but pork is sold (by tradition, the *charcuterie* handles pork). Closed Mondays.

Boucherie chevaline: the horse's head outside shows that this is a horse butcher. Open Mondays.

Boulangerie: perhaps the most important of all, since the French buy their bread fresh twice a day for lunch and dinner. The long, familiar loaf is a *baguette* but *pain complet* (wholemeal bread) is common nowadays, as is *pain de campagne*, a heavy white country bread or *pain de seigle*, a slightly sour rye bread, good with cheese. The sign '*dépôt de pain*' denotes shops that sell bread, but do not bake it.

Charcuterie: formerly the *charcutier* dealt only with the pig and its by-products such as sausages, terrines and pâtés. Nowadays this looks more and more like a delicatessen.

Confiserie: sells sweets made on the premises. Chocolates are always a feature ... and are always beautifully displayed and wrapped.

Épicerie: literally a spice shop, but nowadays the grocer's, carrying almost everything.

Fromagerie: the best cheese shops are run by *affineurs*, who mature cheeses they buy from the farmer and sell them at peak condition.

Pâtisserie: cake shops full of home-made tarts and ice-cream, pastries and cakes. Many have home-made chocolates too.

Poissonnerie: the best fishmongers often smoke fish and make fish pâtés and fish soup.

Street scene with pavement produce, Beuzeville

Signs like this one in Beuvron-en-Auge confirm the individual character of some establishments

Traiteur: ready-made dishes to take home.

Triperie: common in Normandy, where tripe is a popular delicacy, and often tastes better when cooked by a specialist.

Volailler: poulterers seem to be on the decline, since butchers often sell chickens and guinea fowl, roasting them in electric *rôtissoires* for instant take-aways.

Where to find the best
Deauville
La Ferme Normande has all that is best in Normandy food from calvados to cheeses. Right across from the market.
Place du Marché. Tel: 02 31 88 17 86.

Dieppe
L'Épicier Olivier is a delightful delicatessen run by the brother of Philippe Olivier, the famous cheese-shop owner in Boulogne.
16 rue Saint-Jacques. Tel: 02 35 84 22 55.

Etretat
The restored covered market has an assortment of fun shops, including local foods and gifts like unusual candles.

Honfleur
La Paneterie is rated as one of the finest bakeries in Normandy thanks to the efforts of Louis David who bakes at least 15 different breads every day. Purists insist on *pain brié*, a local heavy white bread to accompany shrimps. You can feel his seven-grain loaves doing you the world of good.
Rue de la République. Tel: 02 31 89 18 70.

Pont-Audemer
Le Fromage Blanc is the sort of shop photographers love to spend time in, with discs of real Camembert and Livarot, the square Pont-l'Évêque and cheeses from Bray. Good selection of wines.
21 rue de la République. Tel: 02 32 41 06 79.

Pont-l'Évêque
M Lemonier is an outstanding *boulanger*, with a splendid selection of breads and rolls for sale.
61 rue St-Michel. Tel: 02 31 64 01 94.

Rouen
Hardy is one of the city's most famous old *charcuteries*.
22 place du Vieux Marché. Tel: 02 35 71 81 55.

Despite their love of food and tradition, the French are also conscious of the time and money saved at supermarkets. The result is the *hyper, hypermarché* or hypermarket, the biggest shopping arenas in Europe. The names are splattered across advertising hoardings for miles: Auchan, Carrefour, Champion, Géant Casino, Euromarché, Leclerc and Mammouth.

Farmhouse Fare

*O*ne of the great delights in Normandy is going to see cheeses being made, cider being bottled or calvados distilled ... then buying from the man or woman who produced them. Here is a selection where visitors are welcome: a pair of wellington boots is recommended in wet weather as many are on real working farms. It is worth telephoning to make sure the farmer or his family is there to greet you. Don't be worried if your French is not fluent: an interest in good food transcends language barriers.

CHEESE
Camembert
François Durand's Ferme de la Héronière is in the village that gave its name to the world-famous cheese.
Tel: 02 33 39 08 08.

Boissey
At Fromages des Traditions, at La Houssaye, they not only make cheeses (Livarot, Pont-l'Évêque, Pavé d'Auge) in the old-fashioned way, but sell them directo to the public on weekdays.
Tel: 02 31 20 64 00.

Pont-l'Évêque
At the Fromager de Pont l'Évêque there are free guided tours, year-round. Taste

Choose your cheese with care, and there's no better place to do that than on a farm where it's made

and then buy direct from the makers.
Tel: 02 31 64 61 96.

Cambremer
The Domaine de St-Loup specialises in Camembert on a farm at St-Loup-de-Fribois, just outside Cambremer.
Tel: 02 31 63 04 04.

Livarot
The name Graindorge is synonymous with quality Pont-l'Évêque and Livarot cheeses. Open: Monday to Saturday mornings, April to September.
Tel: 02 31 48 20 10.

St-Hilaire-Petitville
Eric Robert makes cheeses at the Chevrerie du Mesnil in the Cotentin marshes.
Tel: 02 33 42 32 00.

It's tempting to buy just for the labels ...

CIDER AND CALVADOS MAKERS
Crouttes
Just outside Vimoutiers, the Olivier family make excellent *pommeau*, as well as cider and calvados in an old farmhouse.
La Galotière. Tel: 02 33 39 05 98.

Amay-sur-Seulles
In the heart of Calvados, the Aubrée family shows visitors how apple-based drinks are made. With 20 hectares of apple orchards, M Aubrée produces cider and apple juice, *pommeau*, calvados and apple vinegar. A tour includes a visit to the cellars where the drinks are aged, a tasting and entry to a small museum.
Orval. Tel: 02 31 77 02 87.

Dampierre
The Lair family have old agricultural implements as well as tastings for sparkling cider and calvados.
Le Pressoir Dajon. Tel: 02 31 68 72 30.

Farmers such as this preserve the landscapes and flavours of Normandy

Markets

*T*he Normans are great hagglers. That news may come as no comfort for non-French speakers, but a smile, a shrug and a pleading look could help in the markets which thrive all over Normandy.

As in the rest of France, pride of place goes to food, and local produce is of a very high standard: farm-reared chickens and rabbits; farm-made cheese and cider; farm-grown potatoes and carrots; farm-bottled honey and jam. The markets are usually once a week and although local farmers and their wives are regulars, so too are an itinerant band of salespeople with their vans of clothes and shoes, baskets and kitchenware. They follow a circuit, so don't be surprised to see them day after day in market after market. Typical country markets, like those below, are morning-only affairs.

L'Aigle
Tuesday; one of the largest in France with over 1,000 animals as well as local produce.

Alençon
Tuesday
Thursday,
Saturday,
Sunday.
Avranches
Saturday.
Barneville
Saturday.
Carteret
Thursday in summer.
Bayeux
Saturday, place St-Patrice.
Bernay Saturday.
Cabourg Wednesday, Sunday in winter. Daily July, August.

Norman markets are full of excellent produce, but get there early for the very best

Caen
Friday, place St-Sauveur; Sunday, place Courtonne.
Caudebec-en-Caux
Saturday.
Cherbourg
Fish – daily except Sunday; Sunday, avenue de Normandie, Octeville.
Coutances
Thursday.

Dieppe
Saturday.
Etretat
Thursday.
Fécamp
Saturday.
Livarot
Thursday.
Lyons-la-Forêt
Thursday.
Mortagne-sur-Perche
Saturday.
Pont-Audemer
Monday; also Sunday in summer.
Pont-l'Évêque
Monday.
St-Lô
Saturday.
Ste-Mère-Église
Thursday.
St-Vaast-la-Hougue
Saturday.
Sées
Saturday.
Villedieu-les-Poêles
Tuesday.
Vimoutiers
Monday (cattle), Friday.

Speciality Shopping

Caen, Le Mans and Rouen have all the shops expected of sophisticated cities, from department stores to speciality boutiques, but there are also a handful of towns and villages still renowned for specific crafts.

For lace, head for the Musée de la Dentelle in Alençon or the Abbaye des Bénédictines in Argentan (see page 121). Each town had a different *point* (stitch), while a third design was produced in Bayeux. Examples are sold at the lace school in the Hôtel du Doyen (see page 96).

Also in Bayeux are the Ateliers d'Art de Bayeux, small shops in the place aux Pommes (near the new tourist office) which sell well-made reproductions of traditional lace, pottery and tapestry work.

Vannerie (basket-weaving) is still a feature of Remilly-sur-Lozon, a small village on the D8, off the D900 northwest of St-Lô. Bigger by far is Villedieu-les-Poêles, which lives up to

If you're looking for antiques, Normandy is an excellent hunting ground

its name: 'God's town of the frying pans'. Copper pots and pans are everywhere, coated with robust stainless steel or the more delicate tin, preferred by chefs.

Another local tradition is salt-glaze pottery, made originally for workers to take cider to the fields or to transport butter. Noron-la-Poterie, southwest of Bayeux, is the centre of this craft where you can watch potters at the Atelier Turgis (tel: 02 31 92 57 03).

Rouen is known for its faience (see page 31) and reproductions of traditional designs are everywhere. Near the church of St-Maclou is the Carpentier workshop and shop which continues the 400-year-old tradition of hand-painting (26, rue St-Romain: tel: 02 35 88 77 47.) All around this medieval area, the Quartier St-Maclou, are antique shops, rivalled only by the rue St-Pierre in Caen.

Gleaming copper in a specialist shop at Villedieu-les-Poêles

Antiques

Normandy is famous for the richness and depth of its antiques trade. As well as shops, regular auctions take place at the *Salle* or *Hôtel des Ventes* (public auction room).

Parisians like nothing better on a weekend than to poke around the *marchés des puces* (flea markets) looking for bargains. For foreign visitors, these can often be the source of an unusual souvenir.

Look out for the *Salons des Antiquaires* or *Brocanteurs* (antiques or bric-à-brac fair), or even a *Foire aux Affaires*, the equivalent of a carboot sale or garage sale. These tend to be during the winter months.

Duclair – Sunday afternoon in the Salle des Ventes.

Granville – auctions every weekend, but check which day it's on (tel: 02 33 40 03 01).

Le Mans – Friday morning, the flea market is in the avenue de Paderborn below the cathedral.

Nogent-le-Rotrou – the Saturday auction is in the Hôtel des Ventes du Perche.

Rouen – some 100 sellers gather at the Clos St-Marc each weekend near the church of St-Maclou. Be there early. The Thursday flea market is a tradition at the place des Emmurées, muddled in with the usual food and vegetable market. In the third week of October, one of France's largest antiques fairs is in the Parc des Expositions.

Vire – public sales at the Hôtel des Ventes on Saturday afternoons.

Entertainment

*E*ntertainment in Normandy does not revolve around theatre and opera. With such a rural tradition, Normans get together at horse fairs and cattle sales, for festivals of herring and agricultural shows. The weekly market is as much a social as a commercial event.

As for music, there are chamber music concerts and organ recitals in many of the famous churches and abbeys, while summer brings the jazz festival at the Abbaye de l'Épau near Le Mans and the Semaines Musicales (musical weeks) in Fécamp.

Also in summer you can enjoy *Les Imaginaires du Mont-St-Michel*. These are not guided tours; visitors stroll informally through the crypt, cloister and church where light, shadow and music create a special experience.
Tel: 02 33 60 14 30. Nightly except Sunday, early June to September. Admission charge.

Casinos

Good restaurants, discos and floor shows complement the gambling facilities in many French casinos. All are open year round. The most popular game is *boule*, known as '*la roulette des pauvres*' (roulette for the poor). There are only nine numbers; put your *jeton* (chip) on the right number and get back seven times your *mise* (stake). Red or black, odd or even pays even money. There is a minimum 5 FF stake; a maximum 500 FF in most casinos.

Deauville

The most famous casino of them all, the Casino Royal of the James Bond book. Slot machines, *boule*, baccarat, roulette, blackjack and chemin-de-fer.
Tel: 02 31 14 31 14.

Ouistreham–Riva-Bella

At Le Queen Normandy: *boule*, slot machines, nightclub, billiards.
Tel: 02 31 36 30 00.

Trouville-sur-Mer

Blackjack, roulette, *boule*, craps, 200 slot machines.
Tel: 02 31 87 75 00.

FESTIVALS AND EVENTS

Most of the events listed below celebrate the fruits of agriculture; some are modern but others date back hundreds of years.

In Granville, for example, the February Carnival started as a farewell celebration for fishermen about to set sail for the Newfoundland Banks. In Lessay, the Foire Ste-Croix dates back to 1216 and now attracts thousands in September to watch the farmers poke and prod livestock. In Villedieu-les-Poêles, the Grand-Sacré procession commemorates the founding of the town by the Knights of Malta in the 11th century (June, every four years: 1999, 2003).

For an up-to-date listing of festivals, fairs and other events, use the Normandy tourist board website: http://www.normandy-tourism.org.

February:	Sunday before Shrove Tuesday: Granville: carnival.
March:	Mid-month: Mortagne-au-Perche: black pudding fair.

Deauville's elegant casino oozes refinement

April: Middle of month: Le Mans: 24-hour motorcycle race.

April/May: Le Mans: Europa. Jazz Festival at the Abbaye de l'Épau.

May: 1st: Longny-au-Perche: national tripe competition. First Sunday: Lessay: St-Thomas livestock fair. Mont-St-Michel: spring festival. Whitsun weekend: Honfleur: sea festival and pilgrimage to the chapel of Notre-Dame-de-Grâce above town. Check locally: Le Tréport: mussel fair. Ascension Thursday: Etretat: Blessing of the Sea. Ascension weekend: Etretat: festival of Normandy. Check locally: Pont-l'Évêque: cheese festival. Sunday nearest 30th: Rouen: Joan of Arc festival.

June: Middle of month: Le Mans: 24-hour sports car race.

July: First weekend: Fécamp: Festival of the Sea. First week: Château de

Balleroy: Balloon Festival. Mid-month to September: Fécamp: music festival. Last Sunday: Camembert: Camembert Fair. End of month: Granville: Sea Festival. End of month: Mont-St-Michel: beach pilgrimage.

August: First weekend: Livarot: Cheese Fair. 15th: Lisieux: Procession of the Virgin.

September: Beginning of month: Le Havre: Fishermen's Festival. Beginning of month: Deauville Festival of American Films. Second weekend: Lessay: festival of Ste-Croix. Last Sunday: Lisieux: Festival of Ste Thérèse.

November: First Sunday: Dieppe: Herring Fair. First week: Rouen: St-Romain fair. First weekend: Vire: Andouille (sausage) fair.

December: 6th: Évreux: St Nicholas Fair.

DEAUVILLE AND

Eating lunch round the pool at the Hôtel Royal, meeting in the piano-bar at the Normandy or working out at the Hôtel du Golf: celebrities who like to see and be seen at Deauville know where to go. Words like 'elegant' and 'luxurious', 'royalty' and 'film stars' always describe Deauville because, during the summer, this is the Monte Carlo of the North.

TOUJOURS LE SPORT

Sailors come in June for regattas, followed by the racing and horsey crowd at Clairefontaine Racecourse in July, La Touques in August. Bridge lovers and musicians are also July visitors, while the polo World Championship is an August highlight. In September, the film industry invades again, for the Festival of American Films. Throughout the 'season', wealthy families from Paris move in, as they have since the railway arrived in 1863: mother and children are joined by

father for the weekends. No wonder the nicknames of *Tout-Paris-sur-Mer* (Paris Society-by-the-Sea) or the *21st Arrondissement* are popular.

START TIME

The jet-set hovers around the three major hotels. The Normandy has hosted the film stars, ever since Claude Lelouch used this oversized grey-and-white Norman cottage as the backdrop to his 1966 film,

Un homme et une femme – don't be surprised to see Alain Delon in that bar. The old money stays at the Royal, and has done for decades. Racehorse owners and polo players abound, though Kevin Kline and Rosanna Arquette have been spotted in the bar. Out at the Hôtel du Golf with its 27-hole course and tennis courts, racing driver Jean-Pierre Jabouille might rub shoulders with tennis star Henri Leconte. There are balls

THE JET SET

and dinners, nights spent at the Casino, whose tall windows hide over 200 slot machines, plus the strictly-formal Rotonde Restaurant and Régine's nightclub alongside the palatial *salles des jeux* (gambling rooms). Many celebrities have no need of hotels: couturier Yves Saint

Laurent holds court in his seaside mansion; actor Gérard Depardieu lives down the road.

Late risers sip black coffee at Le Bar de la Mer *sur les planches*, then order a seafood lunch near by at Le Bar du Soleil. At Le Ciro's, those in the know ask to see the *Livre d'Or*, the visitor's book, to decipher the autographs of the rich and famous. It's all part of the Deauville season which lasts for a frantic, fun-filled 100 days.

If you want to glimpse a famous face, then Deauville in the season could be a good place to be

Children

*A*lthough Normandy is rich with history, it is still a popular family destination and there are plenty of attractions for younger children when the weather keeps them off the beach. The region is particularly rich in wildlife parks.

Many of these amusement parks are seasonal attractions, open during school holidays. Always check before making your journey.

Balleroy, Château de
The Musée des Ballons (Balloon Museum) reflects France's role in the invention of the *montgolfière* (hot-air balloon). Festival of balloons in June.
15km southwest of Bayeux, off the D572. Tel: 02 31 21 60 61. Open: daily Easter to mid-October. Closed: Wednesday. Admission charge.

Beaumont-sur-Sarthe
The Vieux Moulin de 'Bois Landon': this old mill is still in working order.
23km south of Alençon, on the N138. Tel: 43 97 00 86. Open: all year. Free.

Beauvoir
This reptilarium has 200 snakes and crocodiles from all over the world.
5km south of Mont-St-Michel. Tel: 02 33
68 71 18. Open: daily summer; weekends winter. Admission charge.

Caen-Carpiquet
Festyland is a typical amusement park complete with radio-controlled cars, slides and miniature train.
Just west of Caen, off the N13. Tel: 02 31 75 04 04. Open: daily March to September. Admission charge.

Caudebec-en-Caux
The Musée de la Marine de Seine records the importance of transport on this major river. Good audio-visual display. Many old boats, carefully restored, including a *gribane*, a river transport boat with sails.
35km west of Rouen, on the D982. Tel: 02 35 95 90 13. Open: afternoons daily. Closed: Tuesday September to June. Admission charge.

Eye-catching ceiling in the Château de Balleroy reflects its ballooning connections

Champrépus

The *parc zoologique* (zoo) has nearly 100 species of animals scattered over 6 hectares of Cotentin countryside.
8km west of Villedieu-les-Poêles, on the D924. Tel: 02 33 61 30 74. Open: mid-March to mid-November, daily (closed mornings in winter). Admission charge.

Clécy

The Musée du Chemin de Fer Miniature (model railway museum) is devoted to model and miniature railways with rides (see page 68).
38km southeast of Caen, on the D562. Les Fours à Chaux. Tel: 02 31 69 07 13. Open: Easter to September, daily ; Sunday afternoons only rest of the year. Admission charge.

Clères

This *parc zoologique* is one of the biggest and best in France. Animals including flamingos, emus, kangaroos and antelopes roam freely in the grounds of the Château de Clères.
16km due north of Rouen, off the N27. Tel: 02 35 33 23 08. Open: mid-March to November, daily. Admission charge.

Courseulles

On the seafront, the Maison de la Mer aquarium offers a journey through its glass tunnel to view life under the sea. The fine shell collection is also worth visiting.
18km northeast of Caen, on the D514. Tel: 02 31 37 92 58. Open: daily, except Monday from October to May. Admission charge.

Epretot

Le Canyon is an amusement park with a Wild West theme: water-slides, zoo and games.

15km northeast of Le Havre, off the N15. Tel: 02 35 20 42 69 Open: April to September, Wednesday, weekends; July, August, daily. Admission charge.

Etretat

The Aquarium Marin (Marine Aquarium) at the far end of the Roches Leisure Park has tropical fish as well as local species.
28km north of Le Havre, via the D940. Tel: 02 35 27 01 23. Open: Easter to September, weekends; daily July, August. Admission charge.

La Ferté-Macé

The Musée du Jouet (Toy Museum) brings together toys from the past 100 years and some early sound recordings on wax cylinders
46km northwest of Alençon, on the D916. Rue de la Victoire. Tel: 02 33 37 10 97. Open: weekends April to June, September, October; daily July, August. Admission charge.

Fleury-la-Forêt

The Château de Fleury has a collection of dolls, including a 3m-tall dolls' house and dolls riding a miniature roundabout.
40km east of Rouen, in Lyons Forest. Tel: 02 32 49 63 91. Open: Easter to October, daily. Admission charge.

Gisors

The Parc de Loisirs du Bois d'Hérouval (Hérouval leisure park) is 4km from Gisors on the Pontoise road. With 90 attractions ranging from water-slides to a miniature train, this is always popular with children.
57km southeast of Rouen, on the D14. Tel: 02 32 55 33 76. Open: daily Easter to August. Admission charge.

Peacock and little girl sizing each other up in the park at Clères

Granville

One ticket covers three attractions (the Aquarium Marin du Roc, Palais Minéral, Jardin des Papillons) – see insects, fish, butterflies and the famous 'sculptures' and 'paintings' made entirely from shells.

105km south of Cherbourg, off the D971. Tel: 02 33 50 19 10. Open: February to All Saints', daily. Admission charge.

Grimbosq

The Forêt de Grimbosq contains a wildlife park concentrating on animals native to the region such as deer, wild boar, geese.

16km southwest of Caen, on the D562. Tel: 02 31 30 41 00. Open: daily. Free.

Le Havre

The *Le Havre III* fireship floats alongside the Musée Maritime et Portuaire and is part of the story of merchant shipping. It has been renovated with more work to come. Partially open.

Les Docks Vauban. Tel: 02 35 24 51 00. Open: Sunday, Monday, Wednesday afternoons. Admission charge.

Hermival-les-Vaux

The Parc Zoologique Cerzä, a zoo near Lisieux, has over 250 African animals roaming free in a 50-hectare park. There is also a breeding centre for rare species.

9km northeast of Lisieux, on the D510. Tel: 02 31 62 17 22. Open: daily. Closed: December. Admission charge.

Honfleur

Overlooking the old port, the Église St-Étienne is a 14th-century church housing a good Musée de la Marine (marine museum).

15km northeast of Deauville, on the coast. Tel: 02 31 89 23 30. Open: daily April to September. Closed: Monday April to June, September. Open: weekday afternoons mid-February to March, October to mid-November; all day weekends. Closed: Monday. Admission charge.

Alongside the church above, the Musée d'Ethnographie et d'Art Populaire re-creates the traditional Normandy of yesteryear. Among the dozen rooms are a kitchen with shiny copper pans and a workshop.

Rue de la Prison. Open: see Musée de la Marine above. Admission charge.

Jurques

This *parc zoologique*, the Cabosse Zoo, between Vire and Caen, is another fine example of wild animals roaming free.

On the D577. Tel: 02 31 77 80 58. Open: daily April to September; afternoons in winter. Admission charge.

Le Mans

Musée de l'Automobile, the car museum next to the Le Mans motor racing circuit, has high-tech displays alongside vintage models.

Tel: 02 43 72 72 24. Open: daily. Closed: Tuesday October to May. Admission charge.

Montaigu-la-Brisette

The Parc Animalier St-Martin is a wildlife park with a selection of unusual animals from five continents.

Between Valognes and St-Vaast-la-Hougue, on the D902. Tel: 02 33 40 40 38. Open: daily June to August; weekend afternoons out of season. Admission charge.

Mortain

The Village Enchanté, the Magic Village at Bellefontaine, is both a leisure park and a nature reserve. As well as fairy-tale scenes for smaller children, there is an adventure playground. A model train does the rounds of this fairyland village, which has the added attraction of a puppet theatre. Very popular with the younger ones.

5km northwest of Mortain, on the D33. Tel: 02 33 59 01 93. Open: Easter to September, daily. Admission charge.

Plasnes

The Parc des Oiseaux is a huge bird-life centre with large aviaries set in the forest 4km from Bernay on the RN138.

Tel: 02 32 43 21 22. Open: daily mid-March to end September. Admission charge.

St-Symphorien-des-Monts

Parc St-Symphorien has flower gardens as well as wild animals in these 18th-century grounds. Well worth a visit.

7km from St-Hilaire-du-Harcouët. Tel: 02 33 49 02 41. Open: daily Easter to end October. Admission charge.

St-Vaast-la-Hougue

The island of Tatihou just off the coast now has a maritime museum in the 17th-century fortifications. Cross by boat.

Tel: 02 33 23 19 92. Open: daily May to September; weekends October to April. Admission charge.

Trouville

The Aquarium Écologique is one of France's biggest and best aquariums. Over 20 years old, it boasts mangrove swamps and Amazon rain forest to show off the species in natural habitats. Seventy-five tanks of fish, including several varieties of shark. Also a selection of creepy-crawlies and reptiles.

Tel: 02 31 88 46 04. Open: daily. Admission charge.

Villerville

Mer et Désert complements the aquarium at Trouville with hundreds of live shellfish and cacti.

Between Deauville and Honfleur, on the D513. Tel: 02 31 88 44 06. Open: April to October, daily. Admission charge.

All aboard for fun at Clécy's model railway museum

Sport

Normandy is scarcely a hotbed of sport when it comes to team games like football or basketball. Normans are great individualists; they love horses and horse-racing; they would die to be a great cyclist. One of the sport's legends was Jacques Anquetil who dominated the cycling Tour de France at his peak, winning in 1957 and then 1961 to 1964. Never a showy rider, he ground his opponents down with steady, well-planned riding: gritty and typically Norman.

So Normandy is a place to do sport rather than watch it. The biggest boom in recent years has been golf, catering to the rise in interest across France but also to British, Dutch and German visitors looking for golf without queues.

There are also plenty of opportunities for biking, riding and walking. Renting a *vélo* (bicycle) or VTT (mountain bike) is easy: hire from bike shops, or even from SNCF railway stations at Bayeux, Cabourg, Dives, Fécamp, Le Tréport, Pontorson, Sillé-le-Guillaume, Trouville-Deauville and Vernon. Each *département* has permanent, marked cycle trails.

Hiking trails, too, abound, often linking in to France's national network, the Sentiers de Grande Randonnée, or GR for short. The GR2 runs along the Seine Valley, the GR21 traces the Lézarde Valley and the GR221 cuts through the Suisse Normande. Panoramic views and brisk breezes are a feature of the GR22/223 which follows the coast of the Cotentin Peninsula between Mont-St-Michel and Barfleur.

As for horse-riding, a list of approved establishments is available from the Association Régionale de Tourisme Équestre, rue de la Fontaine Bulante, 27380 Charleval. Tel: 02 32 49 20 48.

Local tourist offices have a wide array of pamphlets for these, and more, activities.

FISHING

Visitors to Normandy have the best of all worlds: sea fishing, fly fishing and coarse fishing. A *gaule* is a fishing rod, a *mouche* is a fly.

Listed below are a selection of the best places to fish. The telephone numbers are for the local fishing associations which look after licences and equipment hire. A knowledge of French is essential.

Sea fish

Anguille: eel
Bars: bass
Cabillaud: cod
Congre: conger eel
Dorade: bream
Mulet: mullet
Raie: skate
Requin: hammerhead shark.

Courseulles

Surf casting for bass and mullet is popular; at the end of the season, in October and November, turbot is available.
Boat hire – tel: 02 31 37 46 80.

Dieppe

Fish from the jetties for conger eels in autumn, from Berneval beach for bass, and from boats for large cod in autumn.
Boat hire – tel: 02 35 84 90 98/35 04 56 08.

Fishing in an incomparable setting: on the Seine at Les Andelys

Fécamp
Bass is plentiful from the jetties in summer, big conger eels in the autumn.
Boat hire – tel: 02 32 28 40 29.

Grandcamp
Off the Pointe du Hoc for bass; flat fish in the Vire estuary.
Boat hire – tel: 02 31 22 64 15/31 21 49 93.

Granville
Between the Chausey Islands and the bay of Mont-St-Michel, skate and hammerhead sharks add to the usual variety.
Boat hire – tel: 02 33 50 37 80.

INLAND FISHING
The chalk streams that run down to the sea are famous for their fly-fishing rivers.
Brochet: pike
Ombre: grayling
Saumon: salmon
Sandre: pike-perch
Truite de mer: sea trout.

Bresle River
On Normandy's northern border, the Bresle is good for sea trout.
Season: late March to early October.
Tel: 02 35 50 12 84.

Charentonne River
One of the best trout streams in Normandy, the Charentonne flows into the Risle.
Tel: 02 32 45 00 28.

Iton River
Évreux is a centre for fly fishing on an 8.5km stretch of the Iton.
Season: late March to early October.

Tel: 02 32 24 04 43.

Marais du Cotentin
Four rivers flow into what used to be called the *pays de l'anguille* (eel-country). Now pike and pike-perch abound.
Tel: 02 33 42 18 34.

Pont-Audemer
Some 6km of the River Risle, a classic chalk stream, offer fair-sized trout (25cm).
Tel: 02 32 41 08 21.

Sée River
Near Mont-St-Michel, this is one of Normandy's top salmon rivers.
Season: early March to mid-September.
Tel: 02 33 49 21 47.

Sienne River
In the southern Manche, the Sienne is best known for its trout, pike and pike-perch.
Season: early March to mid-September.
Tel: 02 33 61 02 47.

Touques River
France's best river for sea trout.
Season: late April to late October.
Tel: 02 31 64 00 77.

Verneuil-sur-Avre
A 5km-stretch of the Avre is open for fly fishing.
Tel: 02 32 32 17 17.

HORSES

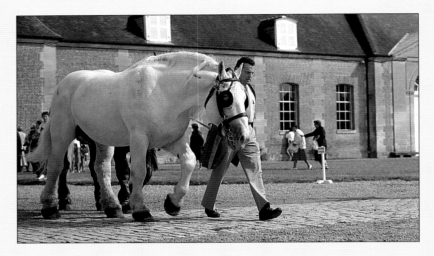

Normandy's love affair with horses goes back centuries, to the days of the heavy horse used by farmers to plough their fields and by knights on the battlefield. During the Crusades, French knights were constantly outmanoeuvred by the swifter and more mobile Arab steeds. When this Arab blood was introduced to France, the quality of local horses improved dramatically.

As early as the 14th century, King Philip VI founded a stud near Domfront, but it was the initiative of Cardinal Richelieu and the minister to Louis XIV, Colbert, in the mid-17th century that launched a national programme of breeding.

The stud at Haras du Pin opened in 1730. The Comte d'Artois (later Charles X) and the Prince de Lambesc went to study English breeding methods, and brought back two legendary stallions, Le Parfait and L'Aleyron. Their offspring

Opposite page: Percheron horses at
Haras du Pin
Left and below: Deauville Grand Prix meeting

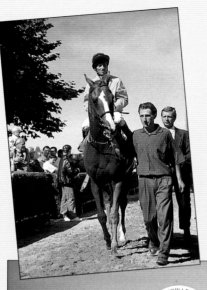

In the middle of the last century,
the English passion for racing was
matched by the French, whose greatest
triumph was that of Gladiateur, who, in
1865, won the English Triple Crown
(2000 Guineas, Derby and St Leger) as
well as the Grand Prix de Paris.

As well as the national studs of St-
Lô and Haras du Pin, there are dozens
in private ownership (over 1,200 in
Calvados alone), easily identified by the
neat white fences and handsome brick
stables.

were so successful that more stallions
were imported; soon Normandy was
the place to buy horses.

Although the network of national
studs with their aristocratic
connections was abolished after the
French Revolution, Napoleon restored
them, realising he needed quality
cavalry mounts to support his
incessant wars.

While the thoroughbred racehorse
receives the greatest publicity,
Normandy also produces high-quality
trotting horses and showjumpers,
steeplechasers and hurdlers. The noble
and massive Percherons have also been
given a new lease of life, delighting
crowds by their ambling gait as they
pull carriages at exhibitions and on state
occasions.

Tee-off practice in an idyllic setting

GOLF

Many regions of France have special golf passes, allowing golfers to play a different course each day. In the Calvados *département*, for example, visitors buying the Golf Pass can play six of the following courses over a period of nine days: Omaha Beach Golf Club; Golf de St-Gatien, Deauville; Golf de St-Julien; Golf de Cabourg le Home; Golf de Clécy-Cantelou and Golf de Caen. The pass is available through Calvados Tourisme, place du Canada, 14000 Caen. Tel: 02 31 86 53 30. The price is lower in the off-season.

The encouragement for visitors can be gauged by the 'minimum handicap of 35 required to play the majority of golf courses in Normandy'.

Agon-Coutainville

Although the Coutainville Golf Club celebrated its 70th birthday in 1995, it is still has only 9 holes. Open all year.
Tel: 02 33 47 03 31.

Bagnoles-de-l'Orne

This elegant spa town needs more than a 9-hole course, but it provides a challenging round.
Tel: 02 33 37 81 42.

Bellême

The 18-hole Golf de Bellême St-Martin attracts a lot of local youngsters.
Tel: 02 33 73 00 07.

Cabourg

Near the spa at Varaville, the Golf de Cabourg le Home has 18 holes.
Tel: 02 31 91 25 56.

Caen

The Golf de Caen is at Biéville. 18 holes.
Tel: 02 31 94 72 09.

Cherbourg

The Association Sportive du Golf de Fontenay has 9 holes.
Tel: 02 33 21 44 27.

Clécy

The Golf de Clécy at the Manoir de Cantelou is a new 18-hole course.
Tel: 02 31 69 72 72.

Deauville

The New Golf Club has been attracting the rich and famous since 1929. 27 holes plus luxury.
Tel: 02 31 14 48 48.

The Golf de St-Gatien at **St-Gatien des Bois** has both an 18- and a 9-hole course.
Tel: 02 31 65 19 99.

Golf Club de l'Amirauté at **Tourgeville** is another new 18-hole course, popular in summer.
Tel: 02 31 14 42 00.

Dieppe

The Golf de Dieppe is the oldest course in Normandy, dating back to 1897. On the Route de Pourville.
Tel: 02 35 84 25 05.

Etretat

Another old course (1908), the Marin d'Etretat has spectacular views from the clifftops, high above the Channel.
Tel: 02 35 27 04 89.

Évreux

The Golf Municipal (18 holes) attracts enthusiastic youngsters. Near the racecourse.
Tel: 02 32 39 66 22.

Granville

The Golf Club de Granville International has been going since 1912. The 27-hole course is open year round, except Tuesdays in winter.
Tel: 02 35 50 23 06.

Le Havre

The Golf du Havre, out at Octeville-sur-Mer, 10km north of Le Havre, has been open for well over 60 years. 18 holes.
Tel: 02 35 46 36 50.

Le Mans

South of the city at Mulsanne, the Le Golf Club du Mans has 18 holes.
Tel: 02 43 42 00 36.

Le Neubourg

The Golf du Château du Champ-du-Bataille is one of the best courses in France, carved out of the woods surrounding the 18th-century château. Open year round.
Tel: 02 32 35 03 72.

Léry-Poses

The Golf de Léry-Poses is a new course in a leisure resort. 18 holes. Open year round.
Tel: 02 32 59 47 42.

Le Vaudreuil

The Golf du Vaudreuil is on an island in the Eure, near Louviers. This picturesque course, with its thatched club house and 18th-century hotel, was designed by English golf guru Fred Hawtree.
Tel: 02 32 59 02 60.

Omaha Beach

The Bayeux Omaha Beach Golf Club with its 27 holes at Port-en-Bessin, is a great success.
Tel: 02 31 21 72 94.

Rouen

The Rouen Golf Club at Mont-St-Aignan is 3km from Rouen. 18 holes.
Tel: 02 35 76 38 65.

SWIMMING, TENNIS AND CENTRES DE LOISIRS

Even the smallest French village will have *camping* (campsite), *piscine* (swimming pool) and *tennis* (tennis courts) to attract holidaymakers. There has also been a growth in the *centres de loisirs* which translates as leisure centres. Often on an artificial lake with a small beach of imported sand, these are ideal for families since they usually offer something for everyone, from pedaloes to fishing, windsurfing to tennis, or, the favourite of the locals, a game of *boules* (French bowls). Some might have water-skiing and special instruction in canoeing or kayaking, a chance to rent mountain bikes or play tennis. There is usually a small café or restaurant.

Brionne

There are lifeguards here in summer.
40km east of Lisieux, on the River Risle, off the N13. Tel: 02 32 43 66 11.

Cany-Barville

Water-skiing is possible on the Lac de Caniel.
20km east of Fécamp, on the D925. Tel: 02 35 97 40 55.

Conches

Tennis and pony rides are among the land-based activities at the Domaine de la Nöé. Summer only.
18km southwest of Évreux, on the D830. Tel: 02 32 30 20 41.

Children learning to sail at Le Havre

Tennis is a popular sport, whether you play or just watch. This court is in Granville

Dangu
With its campsite, this is popular with families who can windsurf and canoe on Gisors Lake.
8km southwest of Gisors, on the D181. Tel: 02 32 55 43 42.

La Ferté-Macé
Based around a huge lake with an imported sandy beach.
46km northwest of Alençon, on the D916. Tel: 02 33 37 10 97.

Grosley-sur-Risle
Visitors have to bring their own windsurfers and canoes, but there is micro-light flying for the daring.
7km south of Beaumont-le-Roger, on the River Risle. Tel: 02 32 46 25 28.

Jumièges-le-Mesnil
A wide-ranging array of adventure sports, include climbing, catamarans and archery.
27km west of Rouen, near the River Seine. Tel: 02 35 37 93 84.

Le Mêle-sur-Sarthe
Water sports and tennis.

20km northeast of Alençon, on the N12. Tel: 02 33 27 61 02.

Pont-l'Évêque
A huge lake for water sports, plus tennis, riding and cycling near the famous cheese town.
47km northeast of Caen, off the A13. Tel: 02 31 64 23 93.

Poses
The Léry-Poses centre is well known for its golf course, water-skiing and campsite.
16km southwest of Rouen, on south bank of the River Seine. Tel: 02 32 59 13 13.

Toutainville
Above-average instruction available at the Centre Nautique for sail sports.
5km west of Pont-Audemer, on the N175. Tel: 02 32 41 13 05.

Vimoutiers
Youngsters enjoy learning to ride at the Escale du Vitou, which has a swimming pool as well as a lake.
27km south of Lisieux, on the D579. Tel: 02 33 39 12 05.

Food and Drink

*T*hree ingredients seem to dominate menus in Normandy: cream, apples and seafood. These are made into cheese and butter, cider and calvados which are cooked with a huge variety of fish and shellfish to present a delicious range of dishes. Pork is also prominent, often chopped up to make sausages and *boudin* (blood pudding). Each area has its specialities, from the duck of Rouen and nearby Duclair to the *pré-salé* lamb of the Mont-St-Michel salt marshes. Tripe is an acquired taste, whether it is served *à la mode de Caen* in a restaurant, or on a skewer from a market stall. A cheese-board should always contain Normandy's cheeses: Camembert and Pont-l'Évêque, goat cheeses and Coeur de Bray. Many desserts include apples or a dash of calvados ... accompanied by a bowl of cream.

Glossary

andouilles de Vire: usually *fumées* (smoked), chitterlings or tripe sausages, served cold in slices as a starter.

andouillettes: smaller tripe sausages, grilled and served hot.

anguilles: eels; sometimes appear in pâtés.

assiette anglaise: assorted cold meats/ sausage served as a starter.

barbue: brill; often served *à l'oseille* (on the bone), in a sorrel sauce.

beignet: doughnut or fritter.

bigorneaux: winkles; served with a pin stuck in a cork.

boudin blanc: white sausage made with white meat such as chicken.

boudin noir: black pudding, sausage made with pig's blood.

bourdelot: whole apple baked in pastry.

brioche: light, sweet bun made with yeast, butter, eggs.

buccins: whelks.

cabillaud: fresh cod; *morue* is salted.

café calva: black coffee with a shot of calvados.

caïeu (d'Isigny): the large mussels from the bay of Isigny.

caneton: duck, duckling. When served *à la rouennaise*, Rouen-style, this duck has pink flesh as it is strangled to keep the

blood. The sauce is very rich.

carotte: carrot.

cassis: blackcurrant.

céleri: celery.

céleri-rave: celeriac: the root is grated and often appears alongside grated carrot in salads as *céleri rémoulade*.

champignon: mushroom.

chaussons aux pommes: apple turnover.

chou: cabbage.

chou-fleur: cauliflower.

ciboulette: chives.

colin: hake; when served *à la granvillaise*, the sauce has shrimps in it.

crevette: shrimp.

criste-marine: samphire.

déca/décaféiné: decaffeinated, as in coffee.

demoiselles (de Cherbourg): often large prawns, but should be small lobsters.

douillon: pear baked in pastry.

Duchesses de Rouen: macaroons.

échalotes: shallots.

estragon: tarragon; *à l'estragon*, with a tarragon sauce.

farci: stuffed.

ficelle normande: stuffed pancake (cheese, ham, mushrooms) in a cream sauce.

fouace: a sweet cake.

fraises: strawberries; *des bois*: wild.

fruits de mer: a mixed platter of fresh shellfish.

gâche: flat, brioche-like breakfast bun.

gades: local name for gooseberries.

gâteau de Trouville: a cake filled with cream and apples.

gibier: game.

groseilles: redcurrants.

groseilles à maquereau: gooseberries, traditionally served with mackerel.

hareng: herring.

huîtres: oysters
   creuses the large Japanese variety
   plates, belons the native oyster
   claires higher class of oyster
   fines de claires very high class oyster, allowed to fatten up in a special *claire* or salt marsh.

jambon: ham; *au cidre*, cooked in cider.

lait: milk.

laitue: lettuce.

lapereau, lapin: rabbit.

lisette: young mackerel.

maquereau: mackerel.

marmite dieppoise: a *marmite* is an old-fashioned cooking pot, but this is a fish stew made with cream, white wine, mushrooms.

matelote normande: a sea-fish stew.

merlan: whiting.

mirlitons (de Rouen): a sort of cream puff.

morue: salt cod.

moules: mussels; *à la marinière*, cooked in white wine, with shallots, herbs and butter; *à la normande*, with cream added to above.

navets: turnips.

oignons: onions.

omelette Mère Poulard: named after the inventor whose restaurant on Mont-St-Michel is legendary. A light, spongy omelette where whites and yolks are beaten separately before mixing.

omelette normande: could be either with cream, calvados and apples (dessert) or with shrimps and mushrooms (starter).

palourdes: clams.

parfum: flavour (as in ice-cream).

persil: parsley.

poireaux: leeks.

pommes de terre: potatoes, often *vapeur* (steamed).

poulet Vallée d'Auge: chicken cooked with cream and cider, even apples.

praires: small clams.

rabote: apple baked in pastry.

radis: radish.

raie: skate.

sablé: shortbread-like biscuit.

salade cauchoise: with potato salad, chopped ham and celery.

sole: sole; *à la dieppoise*, in a white wine, cream and mushroom sauce; often with cream and calvados sauce; *normande*, with cream and cider sauce.

tarte normande: apple tart.

tergoule: rice pudding with cinnamon, also *tord-goule*.

tripes: tripe; *à la mode de Caen*, cooked with cider, calvados and root vegetables.

trou normand: the mid-meal slug of calvados to renew appetite; now often a calvados-flavoured sorbet.

Hand-made *andouille* and its accompaniment, fine cider, at Vire

Restaurants

Price guide
FF under 100FF
FFF under 150FF
FFFF over 150FF

L'AIGLE (AT ST-MICHEL-TUBOEUF)
L'Auberge Saint-Michel FF
Classic rustic restaurant on the edge of the woods.
Tel: 02 33 24 20 12.

ALENÇON
Le Bistrot FF
A 1930s look, old beams, traditional bistro fare.
21 rue Sarthe. Tel: 02 33 26 51 69.
Au Petit Vatel FFF
Michel Lerat is a fine chef; good sauces and imaginative desserts.
72 place Cdt-Desmeulles. Tel: 02 33 26 23 78.

LES ANDELYS
La Chaîne d'Or FFFF
Classic French dishes in a pretty, old inn overlooking the Seine.
27 rue Grande. Tel: 02 32 54 00 31.

BAGNOLES-DE-L'ORNE
Manoir du Lys FFF
Posh hotel restaurant serving local lamb, *crêpes* with apples, even *escargots*.
Rte de Juvigny. Tel: 02 33 37 80 69.

BARNEVILLE-CARTERET
Les Isles FF
Fish dishes served on a terrace overlooking the sea.
9 boulevard Maritime. Tel: 02 33 04 90 76.
La Marine FFF
Lobster, lamb and turbot; pretty views.
11 rue de Paris. Tel: 02 33 53 83 31.

BAYEUX
Le Lion d'Or FFF
Overlooking courtyard of old coaching inn: classic Norman dishes.
71 rue St-Jean. Tel: 02 31 92 06 90.

BÉNOUVILLE
Manoir d'Hastings FFF
Famous restaurant that now seems old-fashioned despite its good, local food.
18 avenue Côte-de-Nacre. Tel: 02 31 44 62 43.

BEUVRON-EN-AUGE
Le Pavé d'Auge FFF
Pretty restaurant in pretty village; good local dishes.
Place Village. Tel: 02 31 79 26 71.

CABOURG
Chez le Bougnat F
Across the river in Dives-sur-Mer, value for money bistro.
27 rue Manneville. Tel: 02 31 91 06 13.

CAEN
La Bourride FFFF
Arguably the best Normandy-style cooking in the region in a luxurious, ancient restaurant.
15 rue du Vaugueux. Tel: 02 31 93 50 76.
Le Rabelais FF
Popular with locals and British for its simple, well-cooked local fare.
Place Foch. Tel: 02 31 27 57 57.

CARENTAN
Auberge Normande FF
Flowery, red-brick roadside inn;

Good company, good weather and good food at Portbail

serves excellent lamb.
17 boulevard Verdun. Tel: 02 33 42 28 28.

CHERBOURG
Le Faitout FF
Busy little bistro, plenty of seafood,
good desserts.
Rue Tour-Carré. Tel: 02 33 04 25 04.

COLLEVILLE-MONTGOMERY
La Ferme Saint-Hubert FF
Traditional dishes from all over France
pack in visitors to the seaside.
3 rue Mer. Tel: 02 31 96 35 41.

CUVES
Le Moulin de Jean FF
Popular London chef Jean-Christophe
Novelli has opened a 'branch' here.
La Lande, Cuves. Tel: 02 33 48 39 29.

DEAUVILLE
Le Ciro's FFFF
Where the superstars lunch and dine
in season overlooking the sea.
Boulevard Mer. Tel: 02 31 14 31 31.
Le Spinnaker FFFF
Up-market Norman dishes include
bourdelot, apple baked in pastry.
52 rue Mirabeau. Tel: 02 31 88 24 40.

DIEPPE
La Mélie FFFF
A real, old-fashioned fish restaurant

right by the old harbour.
2 Grande-rue Pollet. Tel: 02 35 84 21 19.

ETRETAT
Le Belvédère FF
Overlooking the sea; the best dishes are
the local fish.
*11 km south of Etretat. Falaise Antifer.
Tel: 02 35 20 13 76.*

ÉVREUX
Hôtel de France FFF
An elegant hotel-restaurant in the heart
of town.
29 rue St-Thomas. Tel: 02 32 39 09 25.

ÉVRON
Relais du Gué-de-Selle FF
Splendid country restaurant; local
products.
D7, route de Mayenne. Tel: 02 43 91 20 00.

FALAISE AT ST-MARTIN-DE-MIEUX
Château du Tertre FFFF
Luxury country house hotel restaurant
where only the best is good enough.
Tel: 02 31 90 01 04.

FÉCAMP
Le Viking FFF
A nice view of the sea; seafood all the
way on the menu.
63 boulevard Albert I. Tel: 02 35 29 22 92.

GIVERNY
Les Jardins de Giverny FFF
A surprisingly good restaurant, just near
Claude Monet's house.
Chemin Roy. Tel: 02 32 21 60 80.

GRANVILLE
La Gentilhommière FFF
Modern versions of Norman recipes
under ancient beams.
152 rue Couraye. Tel: 02 33 50 17 99.

LE HAVRE
La Petite Auberge FF
Modern versions of old Norman dishes;
popular with locals.
32 rue Ste-Adresse. Tel: 02 35 46 27 32.

HONFLEUR
L'Assiette Gourmande FFF
Chef Bonnefoy creates some daring
dishes with fine local products.
8 place Ste-Cathérine. Tel: 02 31 89 24 88.

HONFLEUR
La Ferme St-Siméon FFFF
The cradle of the Impressionist painters
is a high-quality hotel restaurant today
with appropriately Norman dishes.
Rue A-Marais. Tel: 02 31 89 23 61.

JUMIÈGES
Auberge des Ruines FF
Considering it looks across at the abbey
ruins, standards are high for the regular
flow of tourists.
Place de la Mairie. Tel: 02 35 37 24 05.

LAVAL
La Gerbe de Blé FFF
This hotel restaurant sticks to old-
fashioned dishes and an excellent wine
list: a faultless formula.
83 rue Victor-Boissel. Tel: 02 43 53 14 10.

LE MANS
La Ciboulette FFF
Strictly for fish-lovers, this trendy bistro
is in the old town.
14 rue de la Vielle-Porte. Tel: 02 43 24 65 67.

MONT-ST-MICHEL
La Mère Poulard FFFF
This world-famous restaurant survives
the hordes of tourists who come to order
the fluffy omelettes.
Grande Rue. Tel: 02 33 60 14 01.
St-Pierre FF
This is another good restaurant on the
Mount: excellent value.
Grande Rue. Tel: 02 33 60 14 03.

Watching life go by on the quay of the old harbour at Honfleur

ORBEC
Au Caneton FFF
Big portions of famous local dishes make this half-timbered restaurant a must.
32 rue Grande. Tel: 02 31 32 73 32.

OUISTREHAM
Le Métropolitain FF
Close to the ferry terminal, but serious about its seafood.
1 route de Lion. Tel: 02 31 97 18 61.

PONT-AUDEMER
Auberge du Vieux Puits FFF
Classic, beamed inn with quality food makes this a dream of Normandy come true.
6 rue Notre-Dame-du-Pré. Tel: 02 32 41 01 48.

PONT-L'ÉVÊQUE
Auberge de la Touques FF
Riverside restaurant, half-timbering; Norman classics but only 20 places.
Place Église. Tel: 02 31 64 01 69.

ROUEN
Le Beffroy FFF
A gem in a backstreet thanks to Odile Engel's down-to-earth cooking.
15 rue Beffroy. Tel: 02 35 71 55 27.
La Couronne FFF
Claims to be the oldest *auberge* in France; survives the tourist invasion.
31 place Vieux-Marché. Tel: 02 35 71 40 90.
L'Episode FF
Best value for money in Rouen and fine, imaginative fare, too.
37 rue Ours. Tel: 02 35 89 01 91.
Gill FFFF
Modern, exciting cooking by Gilles Tournadre makes him the top chef in town.

9 quai Bourse. Tel: 02 35 71 16 14.

ST-AUBIN-SUR-MER
Le Saint-Aubin FF
A perfect halt for seafood in the D-Day Beaches tour.
Rue Verdun. Tel: 02 31 97 30 39.

ST-VAAST-LA-HOUGUE
Les Fuschias FF
Imaginative preparation of seafood dishes in this hotel dining room.
18 rue Maréchal-Foch. Tel: 02 33 54 42 26.

SÉES
Le Dauphin FFF
Nice old restaurant in a nice old hotel; good helpings.
31 place Halles. Tel: 02 33 27 80 07.

LE TRÉPORT
Le Saint-Louis FF
Sensibly priced three-course menus for holidaymakers in a hurry.
43 quai François 1. Tel: 02 5 86 20 70.

TROUVILLE
Les Vapeurs FFF
The jolly bistro where the Deauville stars like to slum it. Good fun.
160 boulevard Moureaux. Tel: 02 31 88 15 24.

VIMOUTIERS
La Couronne FF
A useful restaurant near Camembert, serving country dishes.
9 rue du 8 Mai. Tel: 02 33 39 03 04.

VIRE
Manoir de la Pommeraie FF
Local dishes served with a twist of imagination. Garden tables in summer.
At Roullours, 2km southeast. Tel: 02 31 68 07 71.

MILK AND CREAM, BUTTER

Milk is particularly rich in Normandy. The butter from Isigny is exported all over Europe, while the thick *crème fraîche* (slightly soured cream) has an acidity that goes well with sweet desserts.

CAMEMBERT

Normandy's most famous cheese is imitated worldwide, but authentic *camembert fermier* (farm-produced) is made from unpasteurised milk. Two and a half litres of milk go into each 250g flat disk, which is slightly salted before a month's maturation. Boxes labelled AOC (Appellation d'Origine Contrôlée) should contain 'real' Camembert with a rust-red tinge, not the stark white of the factory version. Eaten soft, but not runny, and at room temperature, it is best accompanied by a glass of cider or a soft, fruity wine.

PONT-L'ÉVÊQUE

This is arguably Normandy's oldest cheese, dating at least to the 13th century. Three litres of milk make a 10cm-square block that is regularly washed in cold salted water. Matured for up to six weeks, it has a particularly pungent smell, but the flavour is surprisingly buttery and delicate. Cut it diagonally but do not eat the golden/orange crust. Again, true Pont-l'Évêque bears the AOC. Eat with a strong red wine.

LIVAROT

Another medieval cheese, Livarot is nicknamed the 'colonel' thanks to the five stripes of reed tied round its middle. Five litres of milk go into this strong cheese that can be ripened for some three months. Drink a red wine with it, or a glass of calvados.

AND CHEESE

PAVÉ D'AUGE

Related to Pont-l'Évêque, the *pavé* (paving stone) is bigger, deeper and needs six litres of milk before maturing for three months. The result smells earthy and tastes strong; only a full-bodied red wine can tackle it.

BRILLAT-SAVARIN

Not all Norman cheeses are old. Henri Androuët invented this rich (75 per cent fat) triple cream cheese 60 years ago. Buttery and smooth with a slightly acid

E.GRAINDORGE

FROMAGES D'APPELLATION D'ORIGINE

LIVAROT   PONT L'EVEQUE

or sour aftertaste, this goes well with light, fruity wines, or as its inventor said, with champagne!

LE NEUFCHÂTEL DE BRAY

Production of this cheese takes place only within a 30km radius of Neufchâtel-en-Bray, north of the River Seine. A fresher, less fatty cheese than Camembert, it needs 1 litre of milk for

150g, matured for 10 days. Whether shaped in *coeurs* (hearts), *bondons* or *bondards* (like the *bonde* or bung of a cider barrel) or square *briquettes*, the taste is the same, though some are saltier than others; ask for one that is *pas trop fait* (less salty).

Sampling fine cheese is an essentiall part of any visit to Normandy

Hotels and Accommodation

*A*s a tourist destination since the early 19th century, Normandy's coast has hundreds of hotels. Some are grand and famous like the Normandy at Deauville, others are members of modern chains, dotted round the edges of the larger towns. Then there are the ancient inns that have been receiving guests for centuries, like the Lion d'Or in Bayeux, the burgeoning *chambres d'hôtes* (bed and breakfasts) and, of course, self-catering apartments.

Unless you are travelling during July, August and early September, it is rarely difficult to find a room at the price and standard you require. During the summer holidays, however, advance reservations are essential as most of Paris seems to head for Normandy.

RATING SYSTEM
There are five grades of hotel in France, from the simplicity of one-star to the top

of the range four-star *luxe*, luxury establishment. These stars reflect the range of facilities rather than quality, so a comfortable, friendly two-star hotel may be more to your liking than a more formal four-star hotel which has porters, receptionists and a swimming-pool. The French Government Tourist Office has branches all over the world, often known as La Maison de la France, where full listings of hotels in Normandy are available, as well as suggestions on how to book ahead.

Their annual magazine, *The Traveller in France Reference Guide*, published in Britain, has hundreds of hotel listings along with reservation numbers. Among the most widespread and popular hotel associations are:

Logis de France: some 4,000 family-run hotels in France, mainly in the one- and two-star category. Listed in a book published annually in March.
Tel: 0171 287 3181 (UK); (1) 45 84 83 84 (France).

Châteaux et Hôtels Indépendants: the name spells it out: over 460 independent, comfortable hotels with a special ambience.
Tel: (1) 40 07 00 20 (France).

Hotel with character and to spare: rue Martainville, Rouen

Relais & Châteaux: 150 luxury hotels, often in old castles or country mansions. Illustrated book on sale.
Tel: (1) 45 72 96 50 (France).

Balladins: 80 one-star modern hotels all over France.
Tel: (1) 64 46 49 00 (France).

Campanile: 350 modern, motel-style hotels across France.
Tel: 0181 569 6969 (UK); (1) 64 62 46 46 (France).

Nuit d'Hôtel: over 50 budget-price, modern hotels. No star, but cheap and clean.
Tel: (1) 64 46 05 05 (France).

Ibis–Arcade: 400 modern hotels at two-star level, all over France.
Tel: 0181 283 4500 (UK); (1) 69 91 05 63 (France).

Restotel Primevère: 160 modern two-star hotels, usually on the outskirts of large towns.
Tel: 05 90 85 36 (France, free call).

Once in France, it is well worth stopping at an Office de Tourisme or Syndicat d'Initiative (tourist office) for further suggestions. Some will even help you with reservations.

Chambres d'hôtes

As in the rest of France, this sign has become a familiar sight in Normandy, where more and more private homes are offering bed and breakfast. Some serve just the traditional coffee and bread or croissant, others offer cheese and sausage for German and Dutch tastes. Signs proclaiming 'B&B' or 'English breakfast' indicate just how many British

An establishment making itself known to non-French speakers

visitors cross the English Channel; the Normans recognise that even more are arriving via the Channel Tunnel.

Self-catering

Thousands of French and foreign visitors prefer to rent a cottage and cater for themselves. These include country houses, often with real character and charm. The nationwide Gîtes de France organisation lists all the available properties in a thick, yellow book. It is vital to book several months in advance since holiday periods get booked up, particularly for seaside locations.
Tel: 0990 360360 (UK); (1) 47 42 20 20 (France).

Thomas Cook

Travellers who purchase their travel tickets from a Thomas Cook network location are entitled to use the services of any other Thomas Cook network location, free of charge, to make hotel reservations.

On Business

The French are quite conservative about doing business, especially outside the major cities. Allow plenty of time for appointments and don't try to rush through schemes. The Normans are considered more conservative than most. The best time for an appointment is mid-morning or mid-afternoon. Business lunches may be the way of the world in North America and Britain but less so in France, where meals are considered a social pleasure. Use social meetings to make friendships, to put the client/customer at ease. Avoid broaching business until the coffee stage of a meal.

BANKING

French banking is somewhat different from banking in other EU member nations, and has a reputation for being old-fashioned, slow and stuffy. Outside the major cities, banks are not well versed in dealing internationally. Many overseas visitors prefer to use multi-national banks that have infiltrated France as EU deregulation has grown.

BUSINESS HOTELS

Internationl chain hotels that have the communications facilities required by businesspeople include:

Caen
Holiday Inn City, place Foch.
Tel: 02 31 27 57 57.
Mercure, 1 place Courtonne.
Tel: 02 31 47 24 24.
Novotel, avenue Côte de Nacre.
Tel: 02 31 43 42 00.

Cherbourg
Mercure, Gare Maritime.
Tel: 02 33 44 01 11.

Le Havre
Mercure, Chaussée d'Angoulême.
Tel: 02 35 19 50 50.

Rouen
Mercure, Rouen Centre, rue Croix de Fer.
Tel: 02 35 52 69 52.
Mercure, Rouen Champ de Mars, avenue Aristide Briand.
Tel: 02 35 52 42 32.
Novotel, Rouen Sud Le Madrillet, St-Etienne-du-Rouvray.
Tel: 02 35 66 58 50.

CONFERENCES

Conferences and incentive travel are well catered for with specialist offices in each *département.*

Upper Normandy
Chambre Régionale de Commerce et d'Industrie de Haute-Normandie, 9 rue Robert Schuman, BP124 76002 Rouen Cedex.
Tel: 02 35 88 44 42; fax: 02 35 88 06 52.

Lower Normandy
Chambre Régionale de Commerce et d'Industrie de Basse-Normandie, 21 place de la République, 14052 Caen Cedex.
Tel: 02 31 38 31 38; fax: 02 31 85 76 41.

Pays de la Loire (covering Sarthe and Mayenne)
CDT Pays de la Loire, 2 rue de la Loire, 44200 Nantes.
Tel: 02 40 48 24 20; fax: 02 40 08 07 10.

CONVENTIONS AND SEMINARS

Normandy has a growing reputation for congress and seminar facilities, not only at the traditional seaside resorts but also in the historic cities where many of the older buildings can be hired for special functions. The local tourist offices have full details.

CREDIT CARDS AND TRAVELLERS' CHEQUES

Most French shops and restaurants accept major credit cards. The most popular is the Carte Bleue (part of Visa, Barclaycard and Bank Americard network). However, French franc travellers' cheques seem to be less popular in recent years. Some banks charge a sizeable commission on changing travellers' cheques.

MEDIA

Rouen and Caen are the main publishing centres for press with an economic slant. *La Lettre de la Haute-Normandie* is published every Wednesday, dealing with local economic and political issues. Tel: 02 35 89 78 00.
La Lettre du Développement Local en Normandie is a monthly round-up of local business prospects. Subscription only. Tel: 02 35 89 78 00.
Normandie Magazine rounds up what it calls Anglo-Norman news each month. Published in St-Lô; bilingual English and French. Tel: 02 33 57 28 18.
La Lettre de Basse-Normandie is a weekly round-up of local and political issues published in Caen. Tel: 02 31 75 30 60.

MEETING AND GREETING

The formality of shaking hands is very important. When a group of farmers meet at the market you will see everyone shake hands with everyone else. The same applies in an office; it is advisable

A good start for the businessperson – the local chamber of commerce

to shake every hand on arrival and departure. Always dress formally: suit and tie for men, suit for business women. The French judge a person by the way he or she dresses.

MINITEL

This is a computer keyboard and terminal that hooks into the telephone allowing owners access to thousands of facts and figures, from share prices to the telephone directory.

OPENING HOURS

The two-hour lunch hour is standard throughout France, so days are quite long.
Offices: 8am–12.30pm; 2.30–5pm.
Banks: 9am–noon; 1.30–4.30pm.
(Banks close at noon on the eve of an official holiday.)
Government offices: 9am–noon; 2–6pm.

TELEFAX, FAX MACHINES

Fax machines are commonplace in France. Most hotels, even restaurants, have them so confirmation of bookings is much simpler and more reliable.

Practical Guide

ARRIVING

European Union residents visiting France need only a passport to enter the country. Citizens of the USA, Canada, New Zealand and most other western European nations need no visa unless they intend to stay for more than three months. Australians and South Africans need a visa irrespective of the length of their stay.

Travellers who require visas should obtain them in their country of residence, as it may prove difficult to obtain them elsewhere.

By air

Normandy has five airports with international connections: Caen, Cherbourg, Deauville, Le Havre and Rouen.

By train

Normandy is well served by train, with fast links to Paris, as well as from all the Channel ferry ports and the Channel Tunnel.

By ferry

There are numerous regular ferries from Normandy to the UK: St Malo (for westernmost Normandy), Cherbourg, Ouistreham, Le Havre and Dieppe. The companies are Brittany Ferries, Stena and P&O Ferries.

Irish Ferries have daily sailings in summer from Rosslare and Cork to Le Havre and Cherbourg.

By road

The Autoroute de Normandie speeds visitors and businesspeople through Normandy, starting from Paris in the east, following the Seine to the south, before turning west, and running inland from the coast to Caen where it has been extended towards Bayeux and on to Cherbourg. A toll is payable, dependent on distance travelled.

Many visitors make their way to Normandy by ferry

By rail

The *Thomas Cook European Timetable*, which is published monthly at £8.40 and gives up-to-date details of most European rail services and many shipping services through Europe, will help you plan a rail journey to, from and around France. It is available in the UK from some stations, any branch of Thomas Cook or by phoning 01733 503571/2. In the USA, contact the Forsyth Travel Library Inc., 226 Westchester Avenue, White Plains, New York 10604 (tel: (800) 357 7984 – toll-free).

CAMPING AND CARAVANNING

Normandy has many fine campsites, each graded by the tourist boards who rate the number of facilities on offer, from one- to four-star.

The French love the great outdoors and almost every village has its *camping* (campsite). For detailed information about camping contact the local tourist offices or: Fédération Française de Camping et de Caravanning, 78 rue de Rivoli, 75004 Paris. Tel: (1) 42 72 84 08.

Caravans should maintain a distance of 50m between vehicles, have proper rear view mirrors and be within the maximum dimensions of 11m in length and 2.5m in width.

CHILDREN

Children are a natural and welcome part of any holiday in France. Most can sleep in their parents' bedroom free or for a low supplement. They are welcome in restaurants where children's menus are even more prevalent, as are high chairs. Only the most up-market restaurants would turn a hair at the sight of a family invasion.

When travelling by train, ask for discounts: children under four travel free; from four to 12, half-price.

Men's Suits

UK		36	38	40	42	44	46	48
Rest of Europe	46	48	50	52	54	56	58	
US		36	38	40	42	44	46	48

Dress Sizes

UK		8	10	12	14	16	18
France		36	38	40	42	44	46
Italy		38	40	42	44	46	48
Rest of Europe		34	36	38	40	42	44
US		6	8	10	12	14	16

Men's Shirts

UK	14	14.5		15	15.5	16	16.5	17
Rest of Europe	36	37		38	39/40	41		42	43
US	14	14.5		15	15.5	16	16.5	17

Men's Shoes

UK		7	7.5	8.5		9.5	10.5	11
Rest of Europe	41		42	43		44		45	46
US		8	8.5	9.5	10.5	11.5	12

Women's Shoes

UK		4.5	5	5.5	6		6.5	7
Rest of Europe	38	38	39	39		40	41
US		6	6.5	7	7.5		8	8.5

Conversion Table

FROM	TO	MULTIPLY BY
Inches	Centimetres	2.54
Feet	Metres	0.3048
Yards	Metres	0.9144
Miles	Kilometres	1.6090
Acres	Hectares	0.4047
Gallons	Litres	4.5460
Ounces	Grams	28.35
Pounds	Grams	453.6
Pounds	Kilograms	0.4536
Tons	Tonnes	1.0160

To convert back, for example from centimetres to inches, divide by the number in the third column.

CLIMATE

Normandy's lush green pastures are the result of rain. The damp climate is sometimes warmer than expected, as the Gulf Stream touches the Cotentin Peninsula near Cherbourg. However, with only about two hours of winter sun every day in Cherbourg, it is obvious that summer is the best time to visit. Spring is brisk, autumn mellow with chilly, fire-side evenings ... the winter decidedly raw.

Caen, for example, averages 13°C in April, jumps to 22°C in July and August and slumps back to 15°C in October. The rain comes mainly in the autumn. The best time for touring by car is April and May, when the apple blossom is at its height.

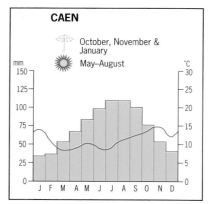

CAEN

October, November & January

May–August

WEATHER CONVERSION CHART
25.4mm = 1 inch
°F = 1.8 × °C + 32

CONVERSION TABLES

See tables.

CRIME

Normandy is quiet and peaceful, but never offer the temptation of visible valuables in the car. At the height of the season, handbags are always at risk in crowds.

CUSTOMS REGULATIONS

There is no limit on the importation of tax-paid goods purchased in an EU country, provided that these goods are for the importer's personal use.

DISABLED TRAVELLERS

Access to the major tourist attractions is improving all the time. However, as most of Normandy's attractions are ancient castles and cathedrals, there are often real problems for wheelchair visitors. Although there are no overall guides for the region, the Comité National Français de Liaison pour la Réadaption des Handicapés (CNFLRH), 236 bis, rue de Tolbiac, 75013 Paris (tel: (1) 53 80 66 66) has leaflets (in French) on aspects of daily life in France.

DRIVING

Driving licences from all European Union countries are valid in France, as are US, Canadian, Australian and New Zealand licences. Drivers should always carry the vehicle's registration documents and valid insurance papers. The so-called 'green card', the International Insurance Certificate, is also highly recommended, as is a home-based breakdown/accident scheme.

Road signs are international. Although *priorité à droite* (priority for cars approaching from the right) still applies in built-up areas, the rule no longer applies on roundabouts. Dipped headlights should be used in poor visibility and, of course, at night. Right-hand drive vehicles should use patches on the headlights to prevent dazzle, though the yellow tinting is no longer a

requirement. If seat belts are fitted, their use is compulsory, as are helmets for motorcyclists.

Car rental is easy in Normandy, with all the major international companies such as Avis, Budget, Eurocar and Hertz represented in the bigger towns; Citer-Eurodollar is a reliable French company.

Speed limits

Urban areas: 50kph
Single carriageway roads: 90kph (on wet roads: 80kph)
Dual carriageway roads: 110kph (on wet roads: 100kph)
Motorways: 130kph (on wet roads: 110kph)
Note: a minimum speed of 80kph applies when overtaking in the middle lane. Motorcycles with less than 80cc have a 75kph speed limit.

Road signs

Rappel is a reminder of speed limit restrictions.
Blue signs indicate motorways.
Green signs indicate main roads.
White signs indicate local roads.
Green signs with *Bis* in yellow are alternative quieter routes.
Yellow signs indicate a *déviation* (diversion).

ELECTRICITY

220 volts is the national standard, along with continental-style plugs. Adaptors are well-worth buying before leaving home.

EMBASSIES AND CONSULATES

Australia 4 rue Jean-Rey, Paris 75015. Tel: (1) 40 59 33 00.
Canada 35 avenue Montaigne, Paris. 75008. Tel: (1) 47 23 01 01.
Ireland 4 rue Rude, Paris 75015. Tel: (1) 45 00 20 87.

New Zealand 7 rue Léonard-da-Vinci, Paris 75016. Tel: (1) 45 00 24 11.
UK 16 rue d'Anjou, Paris 75008. Tel: (1) 44 51 31 00.
US 2 avenue Gabriel, Paris 75008. Tel: (1) 42 96 12 02.

EMERGENCY TELEPHONE NUMBERS

The Thomas Cook Worldwide Customer Promise offers free emergency assistance at any Thomas Cook Network location to travellers who have purchased their travel tickets at a Thomas Cook location. Thomas Cook travellers' cheque refund (24-hour service – report loss or theft within 24 hours) – tel: 0800–90–8330 (toll-free).

General travel assistance for Thomas Cook customers is available from Monde Sans Frontiere, 28 rue de Moscou, 75008 Paris (tel: 331 5342 3854).

Accidents: Police Secours (tel: 17).
Directory enquiries: 12.
European emergency number: dial 112 for direct access to French emergency services.
Ambulance: SAMU (tel: 15) or (tel: 02 35 88 44 22 – in Rouen).
Chemist: ring police for *pharmaciens de garde*/duty chemist.
Dentist: ring police for *dentiste de garde*/duty dentist.
Breakdown: GB Assistance, Caen (tel: 02 31 75 26 00).
Doctor: SOS Médecins: Calvados (tel: 02 31 34 31 31); Rouen (tel: 02 35 03 03 30).
Fire: Sapeurs Pompiers (tel: 18).
Poison: Centre Anti-Poisons, Caen and Rouen (tel: 02 35 88 44 00).

HEALTH AND INSURANCE

There are no mandatory vaccination requirements, and no vaccination

recommendations other than to keep tetanus and polio immunisation up to date. Like every other part of the world, AIDS is present.

Food and water are safe.

All EU countries have reciprocal arrangements for reclaiming the costs of medical services.

UK residents should obain forms CM1 and E111 from any post office in the UK. This provides detailed

---

LANGUAGE
Basic words and phrases

yes	oui
no	non
please	s'il vous plaît
thank you	merci
excuse me	pardon
I am sorry	pardon
good morning	bonjour
good evening	bonsoir
good night	bonne nuit
goodbye	au revoir
I have	j'ai
it is...	c'est
Do you speak English?	Parlez-vous anglais?
I do not understand	Je ne comprends pas

Numbers and quantity

one	un	six	six
two	deux	seven	sept
three	trois	eight	huit
four	quatre	nine	neuf
five	cinq	ten	dix
a little	un peu		
much/many	beaucoup		
enough	assez		
too much/many	trop		

Other phrases

when	quand
yesterday	hier
today	aujourd'hui
tomorrow	demain
at what time...?	à quelle heure...?
where is...?	où est...?
here	ici
there	là
near	près
before	avant
in front of	devant
behind	derrière
opposite	en face de
right	à droite
left	à gauche
straight on	tout droit
car park	un parking
petrol station	un poste à essence
parking	stationnement
prohibited	interdit
bridge	le pont
street	la rue
bus stop	l'arrêt du bus
underground	métro
station	la station de
railway station	la gare
platform	le quai
ticket	un billet
ten métro tickets	un carnet
single ticket	un aller simple

Days of the week

Monday	lundi
Tuesday	mardi
Wednesday	mercredi
Thursday	jeudi
Friday	vendredi
Saturday	samedi
Sunday	dimanche

Months

January	janvier
February	février
March	mars
April	avril
May	mai
June	juin
July	juillet
August	août
September	septembre
October	octobre
November	novembre
December	décembre

information on how to claim and what is covered. Claiming is often a laborious and long drawn-out process and you are only covered for medical care, not for emergency repatriation, holiday cancellation, and so on. You are therefore strongly advised to take out a travel insurance policy to cover all eventualities.

Bird's-eye view of Dieppe

You can purchase such insurance through the AA, branches of Thomas Cook and most travel agents.

HOLIDAYS
1 January New Year's Day
March/April Easter Monday
1 May Labour Day/May Day
8 May VE, Victory in Europe Day
May (mid) Ascension Day
May (late) Whit Monday
14 July Bastille Day
15 August Assumption Day
1 November All Saints' Day
11 November Remembrance Day
25 December Christmas Day
School holidays are staggered so that resorts are not inundated at one time.

LOST PROPERTY
Report anything lost to the local police. For lost or stolen credit cards ring the following numbers in Paris:
American Express – tel: (1) 47 77 72 00
Diner's Club – tel: (1) 47 62 75 00
Eurocard – tel: (1) 45 67 84 84
JCB International – tel: (1) 42 86 06 0 1

Visa International – tel: (1) 42 77 11 90
Thomas Cook travellers' cheques – tel: 0800–90–8330 (toll-free).

MEDIA
Newspapers
Regional newspapers are more influential than the national papers. In Normandy, *Ouest-France* is on sale everywhere.

English-language dailies like *The European*, the *International Herald Tribune* and *USA Today* appear in larger towns alongside popular British dailies.

Radio
Twiddle round the dial to find your choice of non-stop classical music (Radio Classique), pop or ethnic music, all on FM. France Inter on long wave (1829) is the equivalent of BBC Radio 4, which can also be heard quite clearly in Normandy.

Television
France has four state-owned channels and two private channels, but many hotels now have satellite channels piping in English, German and American news, sport and films.

MONEY MATTERS
On 1 January, 1999, the euro became the official currency of France and the French franc became a denomination of the euro. French franc notes and coins continue to be legal tender during a transitional period. Euro bank notes and coins are likely to start to be introduced by 1 January, 2002.

Thomas Cook travellers' cheques free you from the hazards of carrying large amounts of cash, and in the event of loss or theft can quickly be refunded

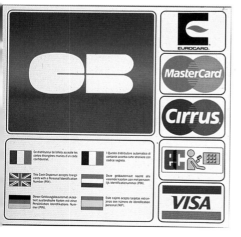

Most credit cards are accepted in France

(see emergency telephone number and emergency help locations).

French franc cheques are recommended, though some banks may charge commission on exchange of these. Cheques denominated in US dollars and other major European currencies are also accepted. Hotels, larger restaurants and some shops in main tourist areas accept travellers' cheques in lieu of cash. Be sure to ask before making the purchase.

MUSEUMS
National museums offer a 50 per cent reduction on Sundays, are closed on Tuesdays, and are free to students under 18. Half-price entry is charged for 18- to 25-year-olds and the over 60s. Municipal museums are free on Sundays, for those under 7 and over 60, and usually close on Mondays. See box on page 22.

OPENING HOURS
Banks: 9am–noon; 2–4pm weekdays. Closed on either Saturday or Monday. Banks close early before a major holiday.
Post offices: 8am–7pm weekdays; 8am–noon Saturdays.
Food shops: 7am–6.30 or 7.30pm. Some open on Sunday mornings.
Other shops: 9 or 10am–6.30 or 7.30pm. Many will close half or all day on Monday, and close from noon–2pm in small towns and villages.
Hypermarkets: stay open until 9pm or later from Monday to Saturday.

PHARMACIES
Pharmacies are often identified by a green cross outside the shop. Contact the police (see emergency telephone numbers) for the duty pharmacist after hours.

Post office

PLACES OF WORSHIP
Normandy is predominantly Catholic, though there are many Protestant churches too.

There are synagogues in the larger towns and cities. Hotels and tourist offices have details of services.

POST OFFICES
Bureaux de poste (post offices) are open Monday to Friday 8am–7pm and Saturday 8am–noon. Stamps can also be bought in a *tabac* (tobacconist). Post boxes are yellow, free-standing or set into a wall.

PUBLIC TRANSPORT
SNCF (French Railways) have reasonable fares and clean trains.

Postcard stand in Lisieux

card) is taking over rapidly. Buy one in a post office or *tabac* to save time, trouble and money. The cards (50 units and 120 units) are much cheaper than a hotel call and simple to use.

Cheap rates operate between 10.30pm and 8am, after 2pm on Saturday and all day Sunday.

In 1996, France introduced new codes. The Paris region retains the (01) prefix; other areas have added 02, 03, 04 or 05. (The 0 is dropped when dialling from abroad.)

For an international call, dial 00, then the country code: Australia: 61; Canada: 1; Ireland: 353; New Zealand: 64; UK: 44; USA:1.

TIME
Normandy is on GMT plus 1 hour in winter, GMT plus 2 hours in summer. When it is noon in winter in Normandy, therefore, it is:

9pm in Canberra, Australia
11am in Dublin, Ireland
11am in London, England
6am in Ottawa, Canada
6am in Washington DC, USA
11pm in Wellington, New Zealand.

TIPPING
Cafés and restaurants include all taxes and tips on their bills. However, after an extended stay at a hotel, it is customary to leave a tip for the chambermaid. Porters, museum guides, taxi drivers and cinema usherettes welcome a *pourboire* (tip).

TOILETS
There are public toilets in department stores, cafés and restaurants, as well as

Fares depend on colour-coded time periods: red, white and blue (the cheapest). Tickets must be validated (*composté*) with a time clock before departure.

Autocars are buses run by SNCF (train fares apply). Regular buses are limited to cities.

SENIOR CITIZENS
Produce a passport to take advantage of any discounts, irrespective of whether or not you are a French national.

STUDENT ACCOMMODATION
Auberges de Jeunesse (Youth Hostels) abound in France. Their French headquarters are at 27 rue Pajol, 75018 Paris (tel: (1) 44 89 87 27).

International handbooks list French hostels for members.

TELEPHONES
Although coin-operated phone booths are common and need a handful of 1 and 5 franc coins, the *télécarte* (phone

the concrete self-cleaning toilettes (coin-operated booths) on the streets.

TOURIST OFFICES

For general information on Normandy contact: Comité Régional de Tourisme, Le Doyenné, 14 rue Charles Corbeau, 27000 Évreux. Tel: 02 32 33 79 00. http://www.normandy-tourism.org

Each *département* has its own head office:

Calvados: CDT, place du Canada, 14000 Caen. Tel: 02 31 27 90 30.
Eure: CDT, Chambre de Commerce, Hôtel du Département, 27003 Évreux. Tel: 02 32 31 51 51.
Manche: CDT, Maison du Département, 50008 St-Lô CEDEX. Tel: 02 33 05 98 70.
Orne: CDT, 88 rue Saint-Blaise, BP 50, 61002 Alençon CEDEX. Tel: 02 33 28 88 71.
Seine-Maritime: CDT, 6 rue Couronné, BP60, 76420 Bihorel-lès-Rouen. Tel: 02 35 59 26 26.
Sarthe: CDT: 40 rue Joinville, 72000 Le Mans. Tel: 02 43 40 22 50.

Mayenne: CDT, BP 343, 84 avenue Robert-Buron, 53014 Laval CEDEX. Tel: 02 43 53 18 18.

TRAINS TOURISTIQUES

You are never too old to enjoy a ride on a train, particularly if it is pulled by a steam engine and chugs through pretty countryside. Check with local tourist offices for timetables.

Alençon to Pré-en-Pail: this line climbs up to La Lacelle station, 302m up in the wooded hills southwest of Alençon.

Connerré to Bonnétable: the Transvap covers an 18km stretch of track in Sarthe.

St Martin-d'Aubigny to Marchésieux: a mini-train rumbles through the marshlands. Halfway between St-Lô and Périers on the D900.

Carteret to Portbail: this coastal run is Le Train de la Côte des Isles.

Caen to Clécy: a popular run through the Suisse Normande via Thury-Harcourt.

Station signpost

ACKNOWLEDGEMENTS

The Automobile Association wishes to thanks the following photographers and libraries for their assistance in the preparation of this book.

ALLSPORT (UK) LTD 118a, 118b, 119 (P Rondeau)
COURTESY OF BRITTANY FERRIES 181
IMPERIAL WAR MUSEUM 87, 88b, 89c
THE NATIONAL GALLERY, LONDON 51a
NATURE PHOTOGRAPHERS LTD 139 (K J Carlson)
PICTURES COLOUR LIBRARY Front cover
WORLD PICTURES LTD Back cover (b)

The remaining photographs are held in the Automobile Association's own photo library (AA PHOTO LIBRARY) and were taken by Rob Moore with the exception of pages 134b, 150, 151, 164 and 167 which were taken by Steve Day; 117 taken by Jerry Edmanson; spine, 13, 18, 19, 22b, 36b, 37a, 37b, 41, 63b, 66b, 90, 96, 105, 107, 109a, 111, 121, 122, 125a, 125b, 128a, 135, 140, 147b, 172 and 175b taken by Clive Sawyer; 174a taken by Barrie Smith; and 149a and 149d taken by Antony Souter.

CONTRIBUTORS
Series adviser: Melissa Shales   **Copy editor:** Audrey Horne   **Indexer:** Marie Lorimer
          Thanks to **Kathy Arnold** and **Paul Wade** for their updating work on this revised edition.